Science 5
Student Guide

Part 2

About K12 Inc.
K12 Inc. (NYSE: LRN) drives innovation and advances the quality of education by delivering state-of-the-art digital learning platforms and technology to students and school districts around the world. K12 is a company of educators offering its online and blended curriculum to charter schools, public school districts, private schools, and directly to families. More information can be found at K12.com.

978-1-60153-341-8

Printed by Bradford & Bigelow, Newburyport, MA, USA, November 2020.

Table of Contents

Student Guide
Lesson 1: Atoms and Elements

How is it possible to know about something that no one can see? These are the challenges faced by scientists who study atoms. We know about atoms because we can see how they behave. Everything is made of atoms, and the way things are depend on the properties of the atoms that make them up. Explore atoms and their subatomic parts.

Lesson Objectives

- Identify the three main parts of atoms as protons, electrons, and neutrons, and that protons have a positive charge, electrons a negative charge, and neutrons have no charge at all.
- Recognize that atoms of each element are exactly alike.
- State that atoms of different elements have different masses depending on the number of protons, electrons, and neutrons, but that most of the mass comes from the protons and neutrons.
- Describe the current model of the atom as a positively charged nucleus containing the protons and neutrons surrounded by electrons moving in certain regions within an electron "cloud."
- Describe the current model of the atom as a positively charged nucleus containing the protons and neutrons surrounded by electrons moving in certain regions within an "electron cloud".

PREPARE

Approximate lesson time is 60 minutes.

Materials

For the Student

   📖 At the Electron Hotel

Keywords and Pronunciation

atom : A tiny particle that is the fundamental building block of any substance. The properties of the atom determine the properties of the element made up of only those atoms.

electron : A tiny part of an atom with a negative electric charge. In an atom, electrons form a cloud around the nucleus.

Erwin Schrödinger (EHR-veen SHROH-ding-ur)

neutron : A particle in the nucleus of an atom, which has no electric charge. Atoms contain neutrons, electrons, and protons.

nucleus (NOO-klee-uhs) : The core of an atom made up of protons and neutrons. Electrons form a cloud around the nucleus of an atom.

proton : A tiny part of the nucleus of an atom, which has a positive electric charge. The number of protons determines the chemical properties of the atom.

subatomic : Particles that make up atoms. Protons, electrons, and neutrons are subatomic particles.

LEARN
Activity 1: Element-ary Science *(Online)*

Activity 2: At The Electron Hotel *(Offline)*
Visit The Electron Hotel to learn a thing or two about how electrons are placed in their own atomic "rooms," called *shells*.

ASSESS

Lesson Assessment: Atoms and Elements *(Online)*
You will complete an offline assessment covering the main objectives of this lesson. Your learning coach will score this assessment.

Name _____   Date _____

At the Electron Hotel

An atom's electrons are arranged in energy levels called *shells*. Which shell an electron is in depends on how much energy it has. Exactly how are these electrons arranged? Let's pay a visit to The Electron Hotel to find out.

The Electron Hotel is a happening place for atoms. It's an especially cool place to stay because there is plenty of room for electrons. Like any hotel, though, there are rules—in particular, at The Electron Hotel there are certain rules for where protons, electrons, and neutrons can be.

Imagine you work at the reception desk at The Electron Hotel. You have been given the following rules for atoms and data for floors. Study them carefully.

Electron Hotel Rules

Rule 1: Protons and neutrons must stay in the lobby (nucleus) at all times.

Rule 2: Electrons must stay in the floors above the lobby. (nucleus)

Rule 3: Each floor can hold only a certain number of electrons.

Rule 4: One floor must be full before you place electrons on the next highest floor.

1st floor	holds	2 electrons
2nd floor	holds	8 electrons
3rd floor	holds	18 electrons
4th floor	holds	32 electrons

At the Electron Hotel

On a cold day, in walks an atom of sodium (symbol = Na). Sodium needs a place to stay. Sodium has 11 electrons. The picture below shows the floors sodium would fill at The Electron Hotel. Notice that the third floor isn't full. That's okay. Count the electrons to make sure there are 11. Then, try placing fluorine (symbol = F) into the hotel.

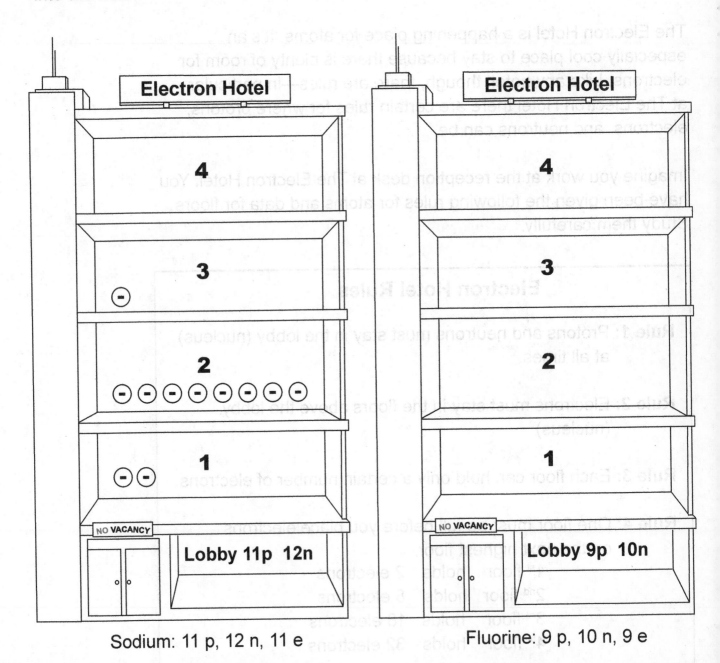

Sodium: 11 p, 12 n, 11 e   Fluorine: 9 p, 10 n, 9 e

At the Electron Hotel

You know that, in real atoms, electrons are not arranged on floors. In the current model of atoms, the lobby is the atom's nucleus and the floors are really energy levels. Electrons move around the nucleus in energy levels, creating an electron cloud. Here's another way to show how electrons move around a nucleus. Study it, then sketch electrons in their energy levels for the following atoms. Stick to the rules of The Electron Hotel!

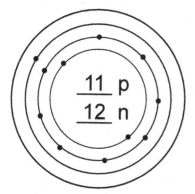

Sodium 11p, 12n, 11e

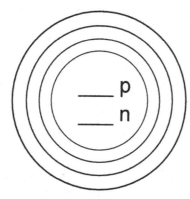

Carbon 6p, 6n, 6e

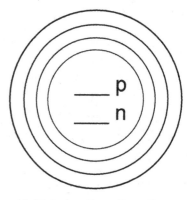

Lithium 3p, 3n, 3e

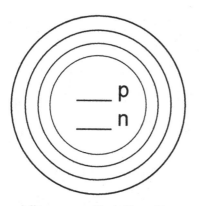

Nitrogen 7p, 7n, 7e

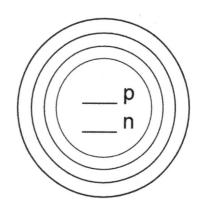

Chlorine 17p, 18n, 17e

Name _____   Date _____

Lesson Assessment

Circle the correct answers and fill in the blanks.

1. What is the difference between two atoms of carbon having the same number of neutrons?
   A. Nothing.
   B. The number of protons.
   C. The number of electrons.
   D. There may be differences in how they react with oxygen.

2. What is the difference between an atom of silver and an atom of gold?
   A. One is new and the other is old.
   B. Their net electrical charges are different.
   C. Their atomic masses are different.
   D. More people would rather have one gold atom than a lot of gold.

3. List the three main parts of an atom and their electrical charges.

   _____

   _____

   _____

4. Describe what the electron cloud model of the atom looks like. Explain where most of an atom's mass comes from. _____

   _____

   _____

   _____

   _____

   _____

Lesson Assessment

Arrange the following electrons into their proper shells.

5.

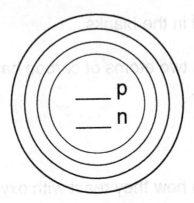

Oxygen: 8p, 8n, 8e

6.

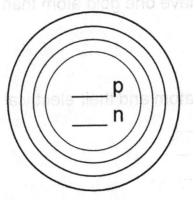

Magnesium: 12p, 12n, 12e

Student Guide
Lesson 2: The Periodic Table of Elements

The Periodic Table of the Elements is a tool that has information on more than 100 known elements. A quick glance at this table and you'll know element names, symbols, numbers, and parts. By the time you finish, you'll be ready to adopt an element of your own.

Lesson Objectives

- Explain that all the elements are organized in the Periodic Table of the Elements according to their chemical properties.
- Find the number of protons, electrons, and neutrons in an atom using its atomic number (the number of protons) and mass number (the number of protons and neutrons).
- Describe the common properties of metals (for example, they have luster, are bendable, and are good conductors of heat and electricity).
- Describe the common properties of nonmetals (for example, they are dull, brittle, and are poor conductors of heat and electricity).

PREPARE

Approximate lesson time is 60 minutes.

Materials

For the Student

🖳 Atomic Calculations

🖳 Periodic Table of the Elements

Keywords and Pronunciation

Dimitry Mendeleev (dih-MEE-tree men-duh-LAY-uhf)

halogen (HA-luh-juhn) : An element that forms a salt when it reacts with other elements. Chlorine, a halogen, reacts with sodium to form common table salt (NaCl).

Jons Jakob Berzelius (youns YAH-kawp buhr-ZAY-lee-uhs)

malleable (MA-lee-uh-buhl) : Able to be hammered out. Aluminum is so malleable that it can be hammered out into a thin foil.

metal : An element that is shiny, a good conductor of electricity, and malleable. Aluminum is a metal.

metalloid (MEH-tl-oyd) : An element that contains properties of both metals and nonmetals. Silicon is a metalloid.

noble gas : An element that is unreactive and rarely forms compounds with other elements. Helium is a noble gas.

nonmetal : An element that is dull, a poor conductor of electricity, and brittle. Oxygen, the most abundant element in the Earth´s crust, is a nonmetal.

LEARN
Activity 1: The Periodic Table (Online)

Activity 2: Atomic Calculations (Offline)
The Periodic Table of the Elements is very useful to scientists because it contains a lot of information in a small space. Use the periodic table to find the number of protons, electrons, and neutrons in an atom of any element.

Activity 3: Adopt an Element (Online)
Make an element your very own! Adopt an element and find out as much as you can about your new chemical friend.

Click the arrow to begin the activity on the next screen.

ASSESS

Lesson Assessment: The Periodic Table of Elements (Online)
You will complete an offline assessment covering the main objectives of this lesson. Your learning coach will score this assessment.

LEARN
Activity 4: More Elemental Stuff (Online)
Did you know that hydrogen once turned a superhero into a proton? Or that sodium was a superhero in a 1963 comic? Look at the Periodic Table of Comic Books to see where elements have turned up in comic book history. Take a quiz on your periodic table knowledge if you're ready.

Safety
The Periodic Table of Comic Books site (referenced in the Beyond the Lesson activity) shows snippets of comic book stories that may include fighting.

Periodic Table of the Elements

Groups: 1 2 3 4 5 6 7 8 9 10 11 12 13 14 15 16 17 18

hydrogen 1 **H** 1.00																	helium 2 **He** 4.00
lithium 3 **Li** 6.94	beryllium 4 **Be** 9.01											boron 5 **B** 10.81	carbon 6 **C** 12.01	nitrogen 7 **N** 14.01	oxygen 8 **O** 16.00	fluorine 9 **F** 19.00	neon 10 **Ne** 20.18
sodium 11 **Na** 22.99	magnesium 12 **Mg** 24.31											aluminum 13 **Al** 26.98	silicon 14 **Si** 28.09	phosphorus 15 **P** 30.97	sulfur 16 **S** 32.07	chlorine 17 **Cl** 35.45	argon 18 **Ar** 39.95
potassium 19 **K** 39.10	calcium 20 **Ca** 40.08	scandium 21 **Sc** 44.96	titanium 22 **Ti** 47.87	vanadium 23 **V** 50.94	chromium 24 **Cr** 51.97	manganese 25 **Mn** 54.94	iron 26 **Fe** 55.85	cobalt 27 **Co** 58.93	nickel 28 **Ni** 58.69	copper 29 **Cu** 63.55	zinc 30 **Zn** 65.41	gallium 31 **Ga** 69.72	germanium 32 **Ge** 72.64	arsenic 33 **As** 74.92	selenium 34 **Se** 78.96	bromine 35 **Br** 79.90	krypton 36 **Kr** 83.80
rubidium 37 **Rb** 85.47	strontium 38 **Sr** 87.62	yttrium 39 **Y** 88.91	zirconium 40 **Zr** 91.22	niobium 41 **Nb** 92.91	molybdenum 42 **Mo** 95.94	technetium 43 **Tc** 98	ruthenium 44 **Ru** 101.07	rhodium 45 **Rh** 102.91	palladium 46 **Pd** 106.42	silver 47 **Ag** 107.87	cadmium 48 **Cd** 112.41	indium 49 **In** 114.82	tin 50 **Sn** 118.71	antimony 51 **Sb** 121.76	tellurium 52 **Te** 127.60	iodine 53 **I** 126.90	xenon 54 **Xe** 131.29
cesium 55 **Cs** 132.91	barium 56 **Ba** 137.33	lutetium 71 **Lu** 174.97	hafnium 72 **Hf** 178.49	tantalum 73 **Ta** 180.95	tungsten 74 **W** 183.84	rhenium 75 **Re** 186.21	osmium 76 **Os** 190.23	iridium 77 **Ir** 192.22	platinum 78 **Pt** 195.08	gold 79 **Au** 196.97	mercury 80 **Hg** 200.59	thallium 81 **Tl** 204.38	lead 82 **Pb** 207.2	bismuth 83 **Bi** 208.98	polonium 84 **Po** 209	astatine 85 **At** 210	radon 86 **Rn** 222
francium 87 **Fr** 223.00	radium 88 **Ra** 226.00	lawrencium 103 **Lr** 262.00	rutherfordium 104 **Rf** 261.00	dubnium 105 **Db** 262.00	seaborgium 106 **Sg** 266.00	bohrium 107 **Bh** 264.00	hassium 108 **Hs** 269.00	meitnerium 109 **Mt** 268.00	ununnilium 110 **Uun** 271.00	unununium 111 **Uuu** 272.00	ununbium 112 **Uub** 285.00	ununtrium 113	ununquadium 114 **Uuq** 289.00	ununpentium 115	ununhexium 116 **Uuh** ???????	ununseptium 117	ununoctium 118 **Uuo** ??????

lanthanum 57 **La** 138.91	cerium 58 **Ce** 140.12	praseodymium 59 **Pr** 140.91	neodymium 60 **Nd** 144.24	promethium 61 **Pm** 145	samarium 62 **Sm** 150.36	europium 63 **Eu** 151.96	gadolinium 64 **Gd** 157.25	terbium 65 **Tb** 158.93	dysprosium 66 **Dy** 162.50	holmium 67 **Ho** 164.93	erbium 68 **Er** 167.26	thulium 69 **Tm** 168.93	ytterbium 70 **Yb** 173.04
actinium 89 **Ac** 227.00	thorium 90 **Th** 232.04	protactinium 91 **Pa** 231.04	uranium 92 **U** 238.03	neptunium 93 **Np** 237	plutonium 94 **Pu** 244	americium 95 **Am** 243	curium 96 **Cm** 247	berkelium 97 **Bk** 247.00	californium 98 **Cf** 251.00	einsteinium 99 **Es** 252.00	fermium 100 **Fm** 257.00	mendelevium 101 **Md** 258.00	nobelium 102 **No** 259.00

Name _____   Date _____

Atomic Calculations

It would be hard to find a tool as useful as The Periodic Table of the Elements. In addition to displaying the name, symbol, atomic number, and atomic mass of more than 100 known elements, the Periodic Table contains much more information that can be quickly read.

In an electrically balanced atom, the number of protons and electrons is the same. The atomic number on the Periodic Table tells you the number of protons an element has in the nucleus of any one atom. Therefore, the atomic number also tells you the number of *electron*s in any one atom. Study the illustration below.

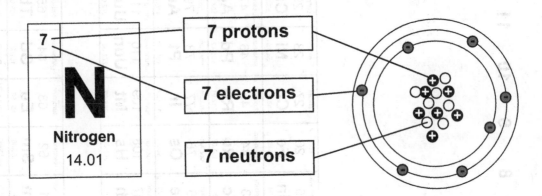

An atom of nitrogen has the same number of protons and electrons. How many neutrons does it have?

Figuring out the number of neutrons requires an easy extra step. At the bottom, under the element symbol, is a number. That number is the atomic mass. Remember that most of the mass in an atom comes from protons and neutrons in the nucleus. Round the atomic mass to the nearest whole number: 14, in this case. Then subtract the number of protons: 7. This number is often close to one or more common isotopes of the element. In some cases, however, an element has many different isotopes and therefore many different numbers of neutrons. The number at the bottom of the square gives you the average atomic mass of all the isotopes.

14 mass – 7 protons = 7 neutrons

Atomic Calculations

Try this for yourself. Color the protons in this oxygen atom. Draw the electrons. Write the number of protons, electrons, and neutrons.

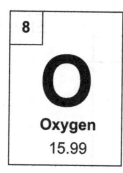

___ protons

___ electrons

___ neutrons

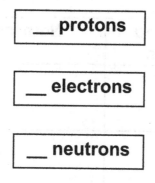

Write the number of protons, electrons, and neutrons in each atom.

Protons: ___
Electrons: ___
Neutrons: ___

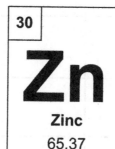

Protons: ___
Electrons: ___
Neutrons: ___

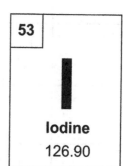

Protons: ___
Electrons: ___
Neutrons: ___

Use the Periodic Table to identify each element. Write the symbol, name, atomic number, and atomic mass in each square.

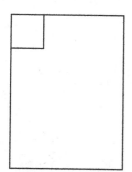

Protons: 29
Electrons: 29
Neutrons: 35

Protons: 14
Electrons: 14
Neutrons: 14

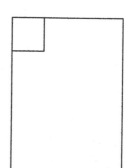

Protons: 82
Electrons: 82
Neutrons: 125

13

Atomic Calculations

Use the Periodic Table to identify each element. Subtract the number of protons from the mass number to find the neutrons.

Atomic Mass (rounded)	Protons and Electrons	Neutrons	Element
12	6		
24	12		
31		16	
59		32	
	17		
197	79		
	88		

Name _____   Date _____

Lesson Assessment

1. What is the Periodic Table of Elements? _____

   _____

   _____

2. Describe three characteristics of metals.

   _____

   _____

   _____

3. Describe three characteristics of nonmetals.

   _____

   _____

   _____

4. Name at least three classes of elements that are grouped
   together on the Periodic Table with similar properties. _____

   _____

   _____

   _____

5. How is it that the Periodic Table is useful to all scientists, no
   matter what language they speak? _____

   _____

   _____

6. Find the number of protons, electrons, and neutrons in one
   atom of neon.
   _____ protons _____ electrons _____neutrons

7. Find the number of protons, electrons, and neutrons in one
   atom of titanium.

Student Guide
Lesson 3: Compounds and Molecules

Elements and now compounds! It takes just over 100 elements to make millions of compounds. Elements join together chemically in special ways. Learn how to read and write a chemical formula and make compound models.

Lesson Objectives

- Use the chemical formula of a compound to identify the elements from which it is composed, and determine the number of each type of atom in the compound.
- Define a *compound* as a substance made of two or more elements.
- Explain that the properties of a compound differ from those of the elements that make up the compound.
- Recognize that elements combine in certain specific proportions to form compounds.

PREPARE

Approximate lesson time is 60 minutes.

Materials

For the Student

📖 Modeling Molecules

Keywords and Pronunciation

subscript : The number displayed to the bottom right of a symbol that tells how many atoms of that element are present in a compound. In the chemical formula H_2O, the number 2 is the subscript.

LEARN
Activity 1: Elements Get Together--Chemically (Online)
Safety

Keep your student away from poisonous products.

Activity 2: Modeling Molecules (Offline)

A chemical formula is used to show what elements and the number of atoms of that element that are in a compound. Study chemical formulas and name the elements in each. Use clay and a key to make models of compounds based on their chemical formulas.

ASSESS
Lesson Assessment: Compounds and Molecules (*Online*)
You will complete an offline assessment covering the main objectives of this lesson. Your learning coach will score this assessment.

LEARN
Activity 3: Surrounded by Compounds (*Online*)
What compounds can be found in a loaf of bread? How about cocktail sauce or shampoo? Search for compounds in foods or products you use each day.

Name_____   Date_____

Modeling Molecules

Write the name and amounts of each element in each formula.

1. NaCl_____

2. H_2SO_4_____

3. $CuSO_4$_____

4. $C_6H_{12}O_6$_____

Write the chemical formula for each molecule pictured below.

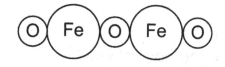

H_2S Fe_2O_3 CH_4 NH_3

C_2H_5OH CO_2 H_2O

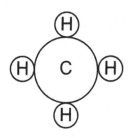

_____   _____   _____

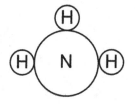

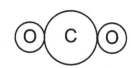

_____   _____   _____

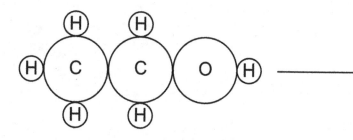

_____

Modeling Molecules

Use clay and the key to make a model of one molecule of each compound. Use resources from this lesson to make sure the atoms are arranged correctly in each molecule.

KEY:
Blue = oxygen
Yellow = nitrogen
Green = hydrogen
Red = carbon

N_2
O_2
H_2O
CO_2
NH_3
CH_4

Challenge Models:
Can you arrange the atoms in the correct way?

C_3H_8
$C_6H_{12}O_6$

Name _____   Date _____

Lesson Assessment

1. What is a compound? _____

_____

_____

2. What happens to the properties of atoms when they are joined through a chemical reaction to form a compound? Give an example. _____

_____

_____

_____

_____

_____

_____

3. What does it mean when a symbol in a chemical formula is not followed by a subscript? _____

_____

4. How is the formula of a compound useful? _____

_____

_____

5. Write the formula for a compound containing one atom of sodium, one atom of oxygen, and one atom of hydrogen. _____

6. Write the formula for a compound containing two atoms of aluminum and three atoms of sulfur. _____

Science - Unit 5: Chemistry,
Lesson 3: Compounds and Molecules.

Name _____ Date _____

Lesson Assessment

1. What is a compound?

2. What happens to the properties of atoms when they are joined through a chemical reaction to form a compound? Give an example.

3. What does it mean when a symbol in a chemical formula is not followed by a subscript?

4. How is the formula of a compound useful?

5. Write the formula for a compound containing one atom of sodium, one atom of oxygen, and one atom of hydrogen.

6. Write the formula for a compound containing two atoms of aluminum and three atoms of sulfur.

Student Guide
Lesson 4: Chemical Reactions

Exploding firecrackers, fizzing antacid tablets, and burning wood. What do these have in common? They are all examples of chemical reactions. Emission of light and heat energy, bubbles, fizzing, and formation of a new solid are all clues that a chemical reaction has taken place. Observe a chemical reaction that produces a green blob and work with chemical equations.

Lesson Objectives

- Identify the reactants and products in a chemical equation.
- Match chemical equations to word equations.
- Recognize that in chemical reactions the original atoms rearrange themselves into new combinations, and that the resulting products have properties differing from those of the reacting compounds.
- Recognize that for every chemical reaction the number of atoms of each element must be the same for both the reactants and the products.

PREPARE

Approximate lesson time is 60 minutes.

Advance Preparation

- Prepare iron acetate. Remove any soap from the steel wool with water. Fill one half of a jar with steel wool. Add vinegar so that is covers the steel wool. Label the jar "Iron Acetate." Leave the jar undisturbed for 5 days.

Materials

For the Student

    💻 Reaction!

    ammonia

    jar - small (2)

    steel wool

    vinegar

    safety goggles

    spoon - tablespoon

    💻 Chemical Equations

    💻 Periodic Table of the Elements

    household item - calculator

    household item - crayons, 64 box

    household item - paper

Keywords and Pronunciation

Antoine Lavoisier (AN-twahn lahv-WAHZ-yay)

LEARN
Activity 1: Chemical Reactions *(Online)*

Activity 2: Reaction! *(Offline)*

If you've ever wanted to be a chemist in a laboratory, this investigation is for you. You won't cure diseases, but you'll cause a chemical reaction that will leave you with a great green blob.

Safety

Wear safety goggles during this activity.

Do not smell, taste, or touch any of the reactants or products.

Wash all remaining solutions down the sink with lots of water after the activity.

Activity 3: Chemical Equations *(Offline)*

Just like math problems, chemical equations show what happens when two or more things are added together. Practice writing chemical equations.

ASSESS
Lesson Assessment: Chemical Reactions *(Online)*

You will complete an offline assessment covering the main objectives of this lesson. Your learning coach will score this assessment.

Name _____   Date _____

Reaction!

Investigate a chemical reaction by joining together two reactants to form a new product.

Materials:
Vinegar
Steel wool
Household ammonia
Tablespoon
Two small jars

LAB SAFETY: Wear safety goggles during this activity. Do not smell, taste, or touch any of the reactants or products.

Procedure:
1. Use water to remove any soap from the steel wool.
2. Label one jar Iron Acetate. Fill it halfway with steel wool.
3. Add enough vinegar to cover the steel wool.
4. Cover the jar securely with the lid.
5. Leave the jar undisturbed for 5 days.
6. Pour 1 tablespoon of the liquid iron acetate into the second jar.
7. Add 1 tablespoon of ammonia and stir.

Observations:
1. Describe what happened during this chemical reaction.

   _____

   _____

2. What clues did you see that told you a reaction had taken place? _____

   _____

Reaction!

The equation for this reaction is:

Ammonium hydroxide + iron acetate $\longrightarrow$ ammonium acetate + iron hydroxide

You can see there was a change of materials but nothing new was produced. The hydroxide, ammonium, acetate, and iron are still there, but the recombination of their atoms produced a completely new substance.

3. What are the reactants? _____

_____

4. What are the products? _____

_____

5. If you were to find the mass of the products and reactants, what differences, if any, would you find? _____

_____

Periodic Table of the Elements

1	2	3	4	5	6	7	8	9	10	11	12	13	14	15	16	17	18
hydrogen 1 **H** 1.00																	helium 2 **He** 4.00
lithium 3 **Li** 6.94	beryllium 4 **Be** 9.01											boron 5 **B** 10.81	carbon 6 **C** 12.01	nitrogen 7 **N** 14.01	oxygen 8 **O** 16.00	fluorine 9 **F** 19.00	neon 10 **Ne** 20.18
sodium 11 **Na** 22.99	magnesium 12 **Mg** 24.31											aluminum 13 **Al** 26.98	silicon 14 **Si** 28.09	phosphorus 15 **P** 30.97	sulfur 16 **S** 32.07	chlorine 17 **Cl** 35.45	argon 18 **Ar** 39.95
potassium 19 **K** 39.10	calcium 20 **Ca** 40.08	scandium 21 **Sc** 44.96	titanium 22 **Ti** 47.87	vanadium 23 **V** 50.94	chromium 24 **Cr** 51.97	manganese 25 **Mn** 54.94	iron 26 **Fe** 55.85	cobalt 27 **Co** 58.93	nickel 28 **Ni** 58.69	copper 29 **Cu** 63.55	zinc 30 **Zn** 65.41	gallium 31 **Ga** 69.72	germanium 32 **Ge** 72.64	arsenic 33 **As** 74.92	selenium 34 **Se** 78.96	bromine 35 **Br** 79.90	krypton 36 **Kr** 83.80
rubidium 37 **Rb** 85.47	strontium 38 **Sr** 87.62	yttrium 39 **Y** 88.91	zirconium 40 **Zr** 91.22	niobium 41 **Nb** 92.91	molybdenum 42 **Mo** 95.94	technetium 43 **Tc** 98	ruthenium 44 **Ru** 101.07	rhodium 45 **Rh** 102.91	palladium 46 **Pd** 106.42	silver 47 **Ag** 107.87	cadmium 48 **Cd** 112.41	indium 49 **In** 114.82	tin 50 **Sn** 118.71	antimony 51 **Sb** 121.76	tellurium 52 **Te** 127.60	iodine 53 **I** 126.90	xenon 54 **Xe** 131.29
cesium 55 **Cs** 132.91	barium 56 **Ba** 137.33	lutetium 71 **Lu** 174.97	hafnium 72 **Hf** 178.49	tantalum 73 **Ta** 180.95	tungsten 74 **W** 183.84	rhenium 75 **Re** 186.21	osmium 76 **Os** 190.23	iridium 77 **Ir** 192.22	platinum 78 **Pt** 195.08	gold 79 **Au** 196.97	mercury 80 **Hg** 200.59	thallium 81 **Tl** 204.38	lead 82 **Pb** 207.2	bismuth 83 **Bi** 208.98	polonium 84 **Po** 209	astatine 85 **At** 210	radon 86 **Rn** 222
francium 87 **Fr** 223.00	radium 88 **Ra** 226.00	lawrencium 103 **Lr** 262.00	rutherfordium 104 **Rf** 261.00	dubnium 105 **Db** 262.00	seaborgium 106 **Sg** 266.00	bohrium 107 **Bh** 264.00	hassium 108 **Hs** 269.00	meitnerium 109 **Mt** 268.00	ununnilium 110 **Uun** 271.00	unununium 111 **Uuu** 272.00	ununbium 112 **Uub** 285.00		ununquadium 114 **Uuq** 289.00		ununhexium 116 **Uuh** ??????		ununoctium 118 **Uuo** ??????

lanthanum 57 **La** 138.91	cerium 58 **Ce** 140.12	praseodymium 59 **Pr** 140.91	neodymium 60 **Nd** 144.24	promethium 61 **Pm** 145	samarium 62 **Sm** 150.36	europium 63 **Eu** 151.96	gadolinium 64 **Gd** 157.25	terbium 65 **Tb** 158.93	dysprosium 66 **Dy** 162.50	holmium 67 **Ho** 164.93	erbium 68 **Er** 167.26	thulium 69 **Tm** 168.93	ytterbium 70 **Yb** 173.04
actinium 89 **Ac** 227.00	thorium 90 **Th** 232.04	protactinium 91 **Pa** 231.04	uranium 92 **U** 238.03	neptunium 93 **Np** 237	plutonium 94 **Pu** 244	americium 95 **Am** 243	curium 96 **Cm** 247	berkelium 97 **Bk** 247.00	californium 98 **Cf** 251.00	einsteinium 99 **Es** 252.00	fermium 100 **Fm** 257.00	mendelevium 101 **Md** 258.00	nobelium 102 **No** 259.00

Name _____   Date _____

Chemical Equations

Chemical equations are a shorthand way of describing chemical reactions. A chemical equation is not finished, though, until it is balanced. A balanced equation has *the same number of atoms on the reactants' side as it has on the products' side.*

A. Count the number of atoms of each element on each side of the equation.
B. Use coefficients to balance the numbers of atoms.
C. Check your work by counting the numbers of atoms on each side of the equation again.

1. $\_H_2 + O_2 \rightarrow \_H_2O$ (water)
2. $\_Na + Cl_2 \rightarrow \_NaCl$ (sodium chloride)
3. $Fe + O_2 \rightarrow \_FeO$ (iron oxide)
4. $\_C + \_H_2O \rightarrow C_6H_{12}O_6$ (glucose)
5. $\_C + \_H_2O \rightarrow C_6H_{12}O_6 + \_O_2$ (glucose and oxygen)

With practice, you can learn to write chemical equations. Read the word equations below, then write their chemical equations. Make sure your equations balance. Chemical formulas that you may need are also listed.

6. Nitrogen and hydrogen yield ammonia.
   Nitrogen: N_2
   Hydrogen: H_2
   Ammonia: NH_3

_____

7. Magnesium and oxygen yield magnesium oxide.
   Magnesium: Mg
   Oxygen: O_2
   Magnesium oxide: MgO

_____

Chemical Equations

8. Bromine and potassium iodide yield potassium bromide and iodine.

      Bromine: Br_2

      Potassium Iodide: KI

      Potassium bromide: KBr

      Iodine: I_2

_____

Challenge

Below is the chemical equation for photosynthesis, the process by which plants use energy from the sun to make food. Rewrite the equation for photosynthesis and balance it, if you can.

$$CO_2 + H_2O + light \rightarrow C_6H_{12}O_6 + O_2$$

_____

Name _____   Date _____

Lesson Assessment

1. In the following equation, which are the reactants and which are the products?

$$2H_2 + O_2 \rightarrow 2H_2O$$

Reactants: _____

Products: _____

2. Match the chemical equations to the word equations.

$H_2 + Cl_2 = 2HCl$ Iron and sulfur react to yield iron sulfide.

$Ca + 2H_2O = Ca(OH)_2 + H_2$ Hydrogen and chlorine react to yield hydrochloric acid.

$Fe + S = FeS$

Mercury and oxygen react to yield mercuric oxide.

$2Hg + O_2 = 2HgO$

Calcium and water react to yield calcium
$CH_4 + O_2 = CO_2 + H_2O$ hydroxide and hydrogen.

3. During this lesson, you observed a chemical reaction between ammonium hydroxide and iron acetate. Describe the properties of the products and of the reactant. _____

_____

_____

4. How do you know when a chemical equation is balanced?

_____

_____

_____

Student Guide
Lesson 5: Acids and Bases

What's sour, corrosive when strong, and contains the element hydrogen? An acid is. What's bitter and slippery when wet? A base is. A substance may be an acid, a base, or it may be neutral. Find out about the properties of acids and bases. Use an indicator and the pH scale to find out if common substances are acids or bases.

Lesson Objectives

- Use the pH Scale to determine whether a solution is acidic or basic.
- Describe properties of acids (for example, acids taste sour, are corrosive, and contain the element hydrogen).
- Describe properties of bases (for example, bases taste bitter and feel slippery when dissolved in water).
- Demonstrate mastery of the skills taught in this lesson.

PREPARE

Approximate lesson time is 60 minutes.

Materials

For the Student

   🖳 Testing Acids and Bases

   ammonia - weak

   aspirin tablet

   cup, plastic (8)

   lemon juice

   litmus paper

   milk of magnesia

   soft drink

   vinegar - white

   graduated cylinder

   soap

   spoon

   tape - masking

   food - head of red cabbage

   strainer - or sieve

Optional

   coffee filter

   household item - food processor or knife

   household item - saucepan or 500 mL beaker

   jar, storage

   rubbing alcohol

Keywords and Pronunciation

base : compound that produces hydroxide ions in solution with water, reacts with an acid to form a salt, captures hydrogen ions, and donates an electron pair to form a chemical bond

acid : A substance that is characterized by sour taste and has a pH of less than 7. Ascorbic acid is found in citrus fruits such as lemons and oranges.

ascorbic (uh-SKOR-bihk)

bases : substance that is characterized by a bitter taste, slippery feel, and a pH of greater than 7

indicator : A dye that can be used to show the pH level of a solution. Litmus paper contains an indicator.

neutralize : To reduce the acidity of a substance with a base, and vice versa. Antacid tablets neutralize the acid in your stomach.

pH : A scale that measures the acidity or baseness of a solution. A substance is classified as an acid if it has a pH of less than 7.

LEARN
Activity 1: Acids and Bases (Online)

Activity 2: Testing Acids and Bases (Offline)

Litmus paper is an indicator that turns red in the presence of an acid and blue in the presence of a base. Use litmus paper to test solutions for this property.

You will need your safety goggles. Do not smell or taste any of the solutions you test in this activity.

Safety

Wear safety goggles. Do not taste or smell any of the solutions used in this activity.

ASSESS
Lesson Assessment: Acids and Bases (Online)

You will complete an offline assessment covering the main objectives of this lesson. Your learning coach will score this assessment.

LEARN
Activity 3. Optional: Cabbage Juice Indicator (Offline)

Follow the directions to make a cabbage juice indicator.

1. Chop the red cabbage.
2. Bring 500 ml water to boil in a saucepan.
3. Add the cabbage to the boiling water and carefully remove from heat.
4. Let the saucepan stand for 30 minutes.
5. Strain the liquid-cabbage mixture and discard the cabbage.
6. For storage, make a solution of the cabbage liquid and alcohol, using 1 part alcohol to 5 parts cabbage liquid. Label carefully to prevent accidents. The cabbage liquid can also be stored by freezing in ice cube trays.

To use as an indicator, add a drop or two of cabbage juice to the substance to be tested. Try re-testing some of the solutions used in the lesson. Observe the color change.

You can also use cabbage juice to make a homemade kind of litmus paper. Another testing method is to soak a filter paper in cabbage liquid. Place on wax paper or paper plate to dry. Cut the dry paper into rectangular strips. The strips can be dipped into substances for testing

Name _____   Date _____

Testing Acids and Bases

Litmus paper is a tool chemists use to determine whether a solution is an acid, a base, or is neutral. It is dipped into a solution and then removed. If the color of the litmus changes to red, the solution is acidic. If it changes to blue, it is basic. If it does not change color, the solution is neutral.

Use litmus paper as an indicator to test for acids and bases.

Hypothesis
From the following list of materials, predict which are acids and which are bases: white vinegar, lemon juice, weak ammonia solution, liquid soap, soft drink, milk of magnesia, aspirin, water.

_____

_____

_____

_____

Materials
litmus paper
8 plastic cups
graduated cylinder
spoon
masking tape
white vinegar
water

lemon juice
weak ammonia solution
liquid soap
soft drink
milk of magnesia
aspirin tablet
eyedropper

LAB SAFETY: Wear safety goggles during this activity. Do not smell or taste any of the solutions you test.

Testing Acids and Bases

Procedure
1. Use masking tape to make a label for each cup: vinegar, lemon juice, ammonia, liquid soap, soft drink, milk of magnesia, aspirin, water.
2. Crush the aspirin tablet in 120 mL of water.
3. Use the cylinder to add 5 mL of each solution to the cups.
4. Use the eyedropper to place a few drops of a solution between your thumb and forefinger, then rub your fingers together. Does the solution feel slippery?
5. Wash your hands.
6. Dip one piece of litmus paper into the first cup. Record your results on the chart.
7. Repeat the test for each cup with a new piece of litmus paper each time.

Science Notebook:
Identify the variables in your experiment. Remember, the *independent variable* is what the experimenter changes in an experiment. The *dependent variable* is what happens because of the change.

Independent Variable: _____

Dependent Variable: _____

_____

Solution	Slippery Feel	Litmus Paper Color	Acid, Base, or Neutral?
White Vinegar			
Lemon Juice			
Ammonia			
Liquid Soap			
Soft Drink			
Milk of Magnesia			
Water			
Aspirin			

Testing Acids and Bases

Conclusion

1. Check your hypothesis. Which substances did you predict correctly? _____

_____

2. If you predicted any incorrectly, explain why you think this happened. _____

_____

Investigation Idea

Wet a cotton swab with your saliva. Touch the saliva to the paper to find out if your saliva is acidic or basic.

Solution	Slippery Feel	Litmus Paper Color	Acid, Base, or Neutral
White Vinegar			
Lemon Juice			
Ammonia			
Liquid Soap			
Soft Drink			
Milk of Magnesia			
Water			
Aspirin			

Name _____   Date _____

Lesson Assessment

Consider the properties of acids and bases. Write True before each true statement. Write False before each false statement.

1. _____ Acids will turn litmus paper red.
2. _____ Acids taste bitter.
3. _____ Bases taste sour.
4. _____ Bases feel slippery.
5. _____ Adding a base makes an acid less acidic.
6. _____ Bases will turn litmus paper red.
7. _____ Ammonia is a base.
8. _____ Acids are corrosive.
9. _____ Acids contain hydrogen.

Tell if the following substances are an acid, a base, or neutral.

10. _____ pH = 11
11. _____ pH = 3
12. _____ pH = 14
13. _____ pH = 2
14. _____ pH = 7

15. Describe how one indicator is used to test whether something is an acid or a base. _____
_____
_____
_____
_____
_____

Lesson Assessment

16. As a scientist, you test a series of solutions to determine their pH. Your results are below.

Substance	pH
A	9
B	12
C	11
D	14

Which one of these solutions would be most effective at neutralizing a strong acid? Why?

_____

_____

_____

Student Guide
Lesson 6: Identification of Compounds

Elements are made of atoms. Elements combine to form compounds. Compounds can combine with other compounds to make even more compounds! Certain tests can be used to determine what elements or compounds are present in the product of a chemical reaction. Try an iodine test for starch and observe flame tests for certain metals.

Lesson Objectives

- Name four types of evidence of a chemical reaction: Change in temperature, color change, release of a gas, and the formation of a precipitate.
- Describe one method of identifying a compound or element in a product of a chemical reaction.

PREPARE

Approximate lesson time is 60 minutes.

Advance Preparation

- If you don't already have it, you will need iodine for the Starch Search activity.

Materials

For the Student

     🖥 Starch Search

       household item - apple

       iodine - Lugol's iodine solution or iodine tincture

       potato - white

       bread

       plate, paper

Keywords and Pronunciation

precipitate (prih-SIH-puh-tayt) : A solid that forms as a result of a chemical reaction. A white solid precipitate may form when aluminum chloride is added to a substance that contains aluminum.

residue : A substance left over as a result of a chemical reaction. The black residue left over from burning fossil fuels or wood is carbon.

LEARN
Activity 1: Identifying Compounds (Online)

Activity 2: Starch Search (Offline)

Searching for starch takes a matter of seconds with iodine. Iodine is a quick reactor to the presence of starch. Look for a color change in iodine to figure out whether a potato, piece of bread, or an apple contain starch.

Safety

Wear safety goggles during the Starch Search activity.

Activity 3: Flame Tests (Online)

Flame tests can be used to figure out whether a compound contains certain metals. It is not safe to do a flame test unless you are in a lab with lab equipment. It is safe, however, to see pictures of flame tests. See three different flame tests and then answer a series of questions about them.

ASSESS

Lesson Assessment: Identification of Compounds (Online)

You will complete an offline assessment covering the main objectives of this lesson. Your learning coach will score this assessment.

Name _____ Date _____

Starch Search

Certain tests can tell whether a particular compound is in a reactant or product. One of those tests is a starch test. Iodine can be used to detect starch in foods.

Hypothesis:
Predict which foods contain starch: apple, bread, and/or potato.

_____

_____

Materials:
1 apple
1 potato
1 slice of bread
iodine
plate

LAB SAFETY:
Wear safety goggles during this experiment.

Procedure:
1. Cut a slice of the apple, potato, and bread.
2. Put the slices on a plate with space between them.
3. Place 2-3 drops of iodine on each piece.
4. Record your observations on page 2.

Science Notebook
The *independent variable* is what an experimenter changes in an experiment. The *dependent variable* is what happens because of the change. Identify both variables.
IV: _____
DV: _____

Starch Search

Observations
Describe how the iodine reacted when placed on each of the foods.

_____

_____

_____

_____

Analysis:
Which foods contain starch? _____

_____

Conclusion:
Describe the method you used to find out whether there was a certain compound in a substance. _____

_____

_____

Investigation Idea:
Some people try to lose weight by eating a low-starch diet. Test other foods of your choice for the presence of starch. Test foods you eat most of the time. Do you have a starchy diet? Are some foods starchier than others?

Name _____   Date _____

Lesson Assessment

Write True if the statement is true. Write False if the statement is false.

1. _____ A change in temperature is always an indicator of a chemical reaction.
2. _____ A color change is an indicator of a chemical reaction.
3. _____ A change in size is an indicator of a chemical reaction.
4. _____ The release of gas is an indicator of a chemical reaction.
5. _____ The formation of a precipitate is an indicator of a chemical reaction.
6. _____ A change in state is an indicator of a chemical reaction.

7. Several methods can tell you whether there is a particular compound or element in a product of a reaction. Describe one method.

   _____

   _____

   _____

   _____

Student Guide
Lesson 7: Molecules of Life

You know that compounds make up the stuff around you, but did you ever stop to think that you are made of compounds, too? Living things contain compounds made from just four main elements. Learn about the three classes of compounds necessary for survival and how you can take them into your body as food.

Lesson Objectives

- Define organic compounds as carbon-based, such as those produced by living things and certain others produced in chemistry laboratories.
- Define inorganic compounds as those that do not usually contain the element carbon.
- Recognize that living organisms are composed of mainly just a few elements: carbon, hydrogen, oxygen, and nitrogen.
- Describe the functions of proteins, lipids, and carbohydrates in human nutrition.

PREPARE

Approximate lesson time is 60 minutes.

Materials

For the Student

- ⬛ Carbohydrates, Proteins, and Lipids
- ⬛ Molecular Models

    clay - blue

    clay - green

    clay - red

    clay - yellow

    toothpicks

Keywords and Pronunciation

carbohydrates (kahr-boh-HIY-drayts) : Substances made from carbon, oxygen, and hydrogen that provide energy to the body in the form of glucose. Pasta, bread, and rice are foods high in carbohydrates.

lipid (LIH-puhdz) : Substances that include fats and oils and provide the body with energy and material to build hormones. Lipids are found in foods containing fat.

proteins : Substances built from amino acids that function in many ways in the body. Proteins provide the body with material for forming new cells, skin, and muscles.

LEARN
Activity 1: The Molecules of Our Lives (Online)

Activity 2: Review Carbohydrates, Proteins, and Lipids (Offline)

Certain compounds are very important to you personally. Your body needs carbohydrates, proteins, and lipids for energy and to carry out processes. Review the structures and functions of these compounds.

Activity 3: Molecular Models (Offline)

Eating is fun--and necessary, too! We must eat in order to get nutrients, such as carbohydrates, proteins, and lipids, into our bodies. Learn how we interact with these organic molecules and build molecular models of each type.

ASSESS

Lesson Assessment: Molecules of Life (Online)

You will complete an offline assessment covering the main objectives of this lesson. Your learning coach will score this assessment.

Name _____   Date _____

Carbohydrates, Proteins, and Lipids

Use the table to compare carbohydrates, proteins, and lipids.
Then answer the questions.

	Carbohydrates	Proteins	Lipids
Structure			
In what foods?			
Purpose in the body			

1. Organic compounds are found naturally in, or are produced by, living things and contain the element _____ .
2. Compounds that do not come from living organisms and do not contain this element are called _____ compounds.
3. What four elements are the main components of living things?

_____

Name _____   Date _____

Molecular Models

Living organisms are made of just a few elements: carbon, hydrogen, nitrogen, and oxygen.

Carbohydrates are made of chains of sugars called *glucose*. The word *carbohydrate* comes from the fact that glucose is made of carbon and water. The formula for glucose is $C_6H_{12}O_6$. A diagram of a glucose molecule is shown below.

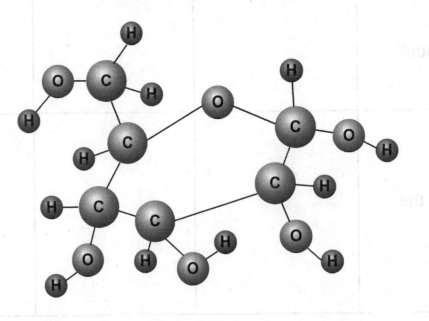

The body uses glucose to make energy. Glucose is a sugar. You may have been told to stay away from sugary foods, such as soda and candy bars, because they make you too energetic. The reason for this is that soda and candy bars contain simple sugars. Simple sugars are absorbed very quickly into your bloodstream, giving you lots of energy quickly. Your body secretes insulin to balance the sugar. A few hours later, your blood sugar drops and you may feel tired and irritable. This describes the "sugar high" and "low" you might feel after eating sweet things.

Molecular Models

Complex carbohydrates take longer to enter the bloodstream. Foods such as pasta and breads contain complex carbohydrates, which are eventually broken down into simple sugars, but much more slowly than glucose breaks down.

When you look at a "Nutrition Facts" label on a food package, look for "Sugars" under the "Carbohydrates" section of the label. This shows the amount of simple sugars the product contains.

Proteins

Proteins are made of chains of amino acids. Amino acids provide your cells with "building material" to grow and develop. They are called *amino acids* because they have an amino group and an acid group. A model of an amino acid is shown below.

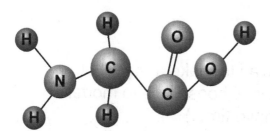

There are two different types of amino acids—essential and nonessential. Your body can make nonessential amino acids. Your body cannot make essential amino acids. You must eat foods that contain them.

Most vegetables are low in protein, but nuts, soybeans, and beans are high in protein. Other good sources of protein are meats, eggs, and dairy products. You can find information about proteins on food labels as well.

Molecular Models

Lipids

Fats and oils are types of lipids. In the body, fats are broken down into fatty acids and glycerol. A fatty acid molecule is shown below.

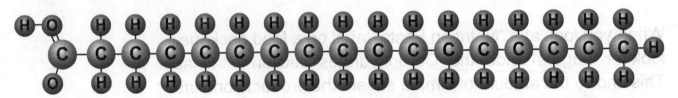

It is important to make fats a part of your diet. Fats are found in vegetable oil, shortening, or lard. These are often used in bread and pastries. Meat has animal fat. Fried food is cooked in fatty oils. Fats are greasy and slick.

Some vitamins will dissolve only in fat, so the only way to get these vitamins is to eat fat. Some fatty acids are essential, and you need them because your body cannot make them. Fats are also good sources of energy.

Make a Model

Use the diagrams, toothpicks, and clay to make a model of either a protein, carbohydrate, or lipid. Choose one to model. (You may do more than one if you have time.)

Red clay = oxygen atom
Blue clay = nitrogen atom
Yellow clay = hydrogen atom
Green clay = carbon atom

1. Compare the glucose and fatty acid molecule. Lipids store more energy in their bonds than carbohydrates do. Explain what happens to the leftover energy. _____

_____

2. Make a list of what you have eaten today. Try to identify each as a carbohydrate, protein, or lipid (fat). Is your diet balanced?

Name _____   Date _____

Lesson Assessment

1. Explain the difference between an organic and inorganic compound. _____

   _____

2. Proteins, carbohydrates, and lipids are which type of compound? _____

   _____

3. Most organic compounds are made of just four elements. What are they? _____

   _____

4. Match the organic compound to its role in nutrition.

   Carbohydrate

   Protein

   Lipid

   a. helps the body build new cells, as well as skin and muscles

   b. provides building material for strong bones and teeth

   c. provides the body with energy in the form of glucose

   d. insulates you from the cold and helps build hormones

Student Guide
Lesson 8: Reaction Rates

Explore four ways by which you can increase the rate of a chemical reaction. Investigate two ways to speed things up--with a plop and a fizz!

Lesson Objectives

- Explain that all chemical reactions require a certain amount of energy in order to break existing bonds in the reactants and form new bonds in the products.
- Recognize that enzymes can act as catalysts to speed up chemical reactions in the human body.
- Identify four ways to increase the rate of a chemical reaction (increase the temperature, surface area, concentration, and add a catalyst).

PREPARE

Approximate lesson time is 60 minutes.

Advance Preparation

- You will need at least 6 fizzling antacid tablets, 3 balloons, and 3 plastic10-12oz bottles for the Quick Action Reaction activity. If you choose to complete the Flour Power activity, you will need a half gallon milk carton and rubber tubing.

Materials

For the Student

    🖥 Quick Action Reaction

        bottle, plastic - 10, 12 oz soda

        drinking glass - clear, 3

        household item - cutting board

        household item - fizzling antacid tablets (6)

        household item - stopwatch

        rock

        thermometer, Celsius/Fahrenheit

        balloon - 3 (blow up to stretch)

        graduated cylinder

        paper

        spoon

        water - tap, cold

        water - tap, room temperature

Optional

> household item - aluminum foil
>
> household item - candle
>
> household item - flour
>
> household item - lighter or match
>
> household item - milk carton, half-gallon
>
> tubing, rubber
>
> funnel

Keywords and Pronunciation

catalyst (KA-tl-uhst) : A substance that increases the rate of a reaction but doesn't get used up. To speed the decomposition of hydrogen peroxide into water and oxygen, use manganese dioxide as a catalyst.

concentration : The amount of something packed into a given space. The concentration of students on the bus increased when Jared and Sonya got on.

enzymes (EN-ziym) : A protein in the body. Some enzymes help break food down into usable nutrients during digestion. Enzymes in your saliva break down starch, starting the process of digestion.

surface area : The amount of space the outer face of an object takes up. To find the surface area of a rectangle, multiply the width times the height.

LEARN
Activity 1: Explore: Reaction Rates (Online)

Activity 2: Quick Action Reaction (Offline)

There are several ways you can speed up the rate of a chemical reaction. Investigate two of them now.

Safety

Wear safety goggles during the Quick Action Reaction activity.

Use caution when handling hot water.

ASSESS
Lesson Assessment: Reaction Rates (Online)

You will complete an offline assessment covering the main objectives of this lesson. Your learning coach will score this assessment.

LEARN
Activity 3: Flour Power--Surface Area and Reactions (Online)

View, or try, an activity that will show the effect of increasing surface area on the rate of a chemical reaction. This demonstration really ends with a bang! Note: This activity involves flames. Do not do this activity without supervision of an adult. This activity must be done in a wide-open area.

Safety

The Flour Power activity involves flames. Please supervise your student.

The Flour Power activity must be done in a wide-open area.

Name _____   Date _____

Quick Action Reaction

Fill in the blanks to review four ways to speed up a chemical reaction.

1. A _____ speeds up a chemical reaction without being used up.
2. Increasing the _____ increases the energy at which atoms collide in a reaction.
3. Breaking up a substance into smaller pieces increases
   _____ .
4. Packing more molecules into a certain space increases the
   _____ of a substance.

Try It!

Dropping an antacid tablet into a cup of water produces a lot of fizz--and a chemical reaction. The reaction of the tablet and water releases carbon dioxide gas. You can use this simple reaction to investigate ways to speed up reaction rates.

Investigation: Temperature and Reaction Rate

You can increase the rate of a chemical reaction by increasing the temperature of these reactants.

Hypothesis: Predict how many times faster an antacid tablet will react in hot water than in cold water. _____

_____

Quick Action Reaction

Materials:
fizzing antacid tablets (such as those with sodium bicarbonate), 6
tap water
clear glasses, 3
balloons, 3 (blow up to stretch)
spoon
10-12 oz (248-340 mL) soda bottles, 3
stopwatch
thermometer
rock
cutting board
paper
graduated cylinder

Lab Safety: Wear safety goggles during the activity. Use caution when handling hot water.

Procedure:
Hot Water
1. Run water from the hot tap until it is as hot as possible.
2. Fill a glass with 150 mL of hot water.
3. Use the thermometer to find and record the temperature of the water, then pour the water into one of the soda bottles.
4. Break an antacid tablet into about five pieces. Add it to the hot water bottle.
5. Have a partner immediately place a balloon over the mouth of the bottle. Start the timer. *Be quick!* The reaction takes less than 15 seconds.
6. Time how long it takes for the balloon to inflate. Record your observations.

Room-Temperature Water
7. Fill a glass with 150 mL of room-temperature water.
8. Repeat steps 3-6.

Cold Water
9. Fill a glass with 75 mL of water. Add ice to adjust the level to 150 mL. Stir the ice water for about 15 seconds.
10. Repeat steps 3-6. Leave the ice cubes in the water.

Quick Action Reaction

Scientist Notebook

Identify the independent variable (what is changed) and dependent variable (what will happen) in this investigation.

_____

_____

Observations

Temperature of Water °C	Reaction Time in Seconds

Analysis

Make a line graph of your data.

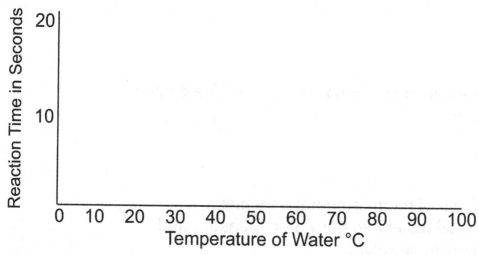

Conclusion

1. What happens to the rate of reaction as the temperature increases? _____

2. How many times faster was the reaction in hot water than in cold water? _____

3. How many seconds would it take for an antacid tablet to react with water at a temperature of 10°C? _____

4. If the temperature is doubled from 20°C to 40°C, the time for the rate of reaction will _____.

Quick Action Reaction

Investigation: Surface Area and Reaction Rate
Increasing the surface area of a reactant by breaking it up into pieces will expose more of the reactant so its molecules collide faster and more often.

Hypothesis: Predict how much faster a ground-up antacid tablet will react compared to a whole tablet. _____

_____

_____

Materials
clear glasses, 3
fizzing antacid tablets (such as those with sodium bicarbonate), 3
rock
cutting board
stopwatch
paper
graduated cylinder

Lab Safety: Wear safety goggles during the activity. Use caution when handling hot water.

Procedure
Whole Tablet
1. Fill a glass with 150 mL of room-temperature water.
2. Drop one whole antacid tablet into the water. Measure and record the time it takes to dissolve.

Tablet in Pieces
3. Place one antacid tablet on paper and break it into about eight pieces of equal size.
4. Repeat step one.
5. Slide the broken tablet from the paper into the glass. Measure and record the time it takes to dissolve.

Quick Action Reaction

Powdered Tablet

1. Use the rock and cutting board to grind one tablet into a fine powder.
2. Transfer the powder into a glass (before adding water).
3. Add 150 mL of water to the glass. Measure and record the time the powder takes to dissolve.

Scientist Notebook

Identify the independent variable (what is changed) and dependent variable (what will happen) in this investigation.

_____

_____

Observations

Condition of Tablet	Reaction Time in Seconds
Whole	
Broken	
Powder	

Analysis

Make a bar graph of your data

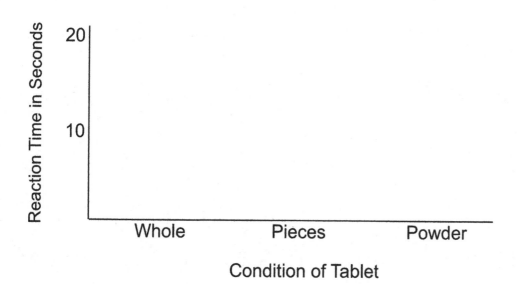

Quick Action Reaction

Conclusion

1. What happens to the rate of reaction as the particle size decreases? _____

2. The rate of reaction for the powder was _____ faster than for the whole tablet.

3. Which has more of an effect on the rate of a reaction—particle size or temperature? _____

_____

_____

Name _____ Date _____

Lesson Assessment

Fill in the blanks to identify ways of speeding up chemical reactions.

1. Add a _____ that is unaffected by the reaction.
2. Expose more of the reactant by increasing the _____.
3. Pack in more of the reactant to increase the _____.
4. Increase the _____ to allow the reaction to happen with more energy.

5. In order for a chemical reaction to take place, a certain amount of _____ must be present.
   A. heat
   B. friction
   C. chemicals
   D. energy

6. Catalysts that speed up chemical reactions in the human body are called
   A. hormones
   B. enzymes
   C. reactants
   D. products

Student Guide
Lesson 9: Unit Review and Assessment

You are familiar with atomic structure and the periodic table. Compounds, chemical reactions, and chemical equations you've also got down. You're ready to show your new skills in chemistry.

Lesson Objectives

- Identify the three main parts of atoms as protons, electrons, and neutrons, and that protons have a positive charge, electrons a negative charge, and neutrons have no charge at all.
- Explain that all the elements are organized in the Periodic Table of the Elements according to their chemical properties.
- Use the pH Scale to determine whether a solution is acidic or basic.
- Describe the current model of the atom as a positively charged nucleus containing the protons and neutrons surrounded by electrons moving in certain regions within an "electron cloud".
- Recognize that in chemical reactions the original atoms rearrange themselves into new combinations, and that the resulting products have properties differing from those of the reacting compounds.
- Recognize that the atoms of an element are exactly alike and that each element is made of only one kind of atom.
- Describe the common properties of metals and nonmetals.
- Identify some common elements and compounds by both their chemical symbols and their formulas.
- Describe a *compound* as a substance made of two or more elements. Explain that the properties of a compound differ from those of the elements that make up the compound.
- Write chemical equations to show what happens in a chemical reaction.
- Explain that all chemical reactions require energy.
- Describe how reaction rates increase with temperature, surface area, concentration, and in the presence of a catalyst.
- Find the number of protons, electrons, and neutrons in an atom using its atomic number (the number of protons) and mass number (the number of protons and neutrons).
- Recognize that atoms of each element are exactly alike.
- Describe the common properties of metals (for example, they have luster, are bendable, and are good conductors of heat and electricity).
- Describe the common properties of nonmetals (for example, they are dull, brittle, and are poor conductors of heat and electricity).
- Define a *compound* as a substance made of two or more elements.
- Name four types of evidence of a chemical reaction: Change in temperature, color change, release of a gas, and the formation of a precipitate.
- Recognize that living organisms are composed of mainly just a few elements: carbon, hydrogen, oxygen, and nitrogen.
- Recognize that enzymes can act as catalysts to speed up chemical reactions in the human body.
- Demonstrate mastery of the skills taught in this unit.
- Identify some parts of the human endocrine system and their function (pituitary gland, thyroid gland, adrenal gland, and pancreas).

PREPARE

Approximate lesson time is 60 minutes.

Materials

For the Student

📖 Question Review Table

LEARN
Activity 1: Professor Pete and the Interview (Online)

ASSESS

Unit Assessment: Chemistry (Online)

Complete the offline part of the Unit Assessment. Your learning coach will score this part of the test.

LEARN
Activity 2. Optional: Unit Assessment Review Table (Online)

If you earned a score of **less than 80%** on the Unit Assessment, complete the activity.

If you earned a score of **80% or greater**, you may skip this activity.

Let's prepare to retake the Unit Assessment:

- Print the Question Review Table.
- Identify the questions that you answered incorrectly.
- Complete the appropriate review activities listed in the table.

Note: This will guide you through the process of using the Unit Assessment Review Tables. You may skip this video if you've already viewed it in another unit or course. As always, check in with your student's teacher if you have any questions.

Activity 3. Optional: ZlugQuest Measurement (Online)

Name: _____   Date: _____

Unit Assessment

Chemistry

Choose the letter that best answers the question.

1. How are elements arranged in the Periodic Table?

   A. by their properties

   B. alphabetically

   C. by how much they are worth

   D. in the order they were discovered

2. Which is the correct symbol for the element *silicon*?

   A. SI

   B. S

   C. Si

   D. Sil

3. All atoms of an element are _____.

   A. flammable

   B. visible under a microscope

   C. alike

   D. different

4. Elements that are usually shiny and good conductors of heat and electricity are known as _____.

   A. gases

   B. metals

   C. solids

   D. nonmetals

5. The most recent model of an atom is the _____.

    A. Bohr model

    B. Plum Pudding model

    C. Cookie Dough model

    D. Electron Cloud model

6. Elements that are usually dull, brittle, and do not conduct electricity are known as

    A. gases

    B. metals

    C. solids

    D. nonmetals

7. Elements join together to form

    A. compounds

    B. ions

    C. protons

    D. atomic masses

8. Which picture best shows an atom?

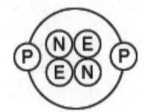

    A.

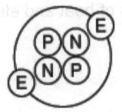

    B.

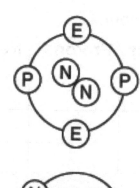

C.

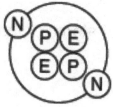

D.

9. In order for a chemical reaction to take place, a certain amount of
_____ must be present.

   A. heat

   B. friction

   C. chemicals

   D. energy

10. Enzymes are _____ in the body that speed up chemical reactions.

    A. catalysts

    B. cells

    C. concentrations

    D. chloroplasts

Answer the questions below by writing *protons*, *neutrons*, or *electrons* on the line or lines.

11. The three main parts of an atom are _____,
_____, and _____.

12. An electrically neutral atom has the same number of _____
and _____.

13. Particles with negative charges are called _____. Positively
charged particles are called _____. Particles with no charge
are called _____.

14. To find the number of neutrons in an atom, you subtract the number of
_____ from the mass number.

15. Fill in the chart with the correct name, symbol, or number.

Element	Symbol	Atomic Number	Atomic Mass Rounded	Electrons	Protons	Neutrons
	Ca					
Boron						

Tell which element is in each compound and the number of atoms of that element.

16. NaCl _____

17. $CoCl_2$ _____

18. H_2SO_4 _____

Write the formula for the compound described.

19. 1 atom of carbon, 2 atoms of oxygen _____

20. 1 atom of copper, 1 atom of sulfur, 4 atoms of oxygen _____

21. 2 atoms of aluminum, 3 atoms of sulfur _____

22. Give an example of how two elements changed properties when they formed a compound.

_____

_____

_____

Tell if the following solutions are acidic or basic.

23. pH = 12 _____

24. pH = 3 _____

25. Write the equation that matches the description.

One atom of zinc reacts with one atom of sulfur to yield one molecule of zinc sulfide. _____

26. Adding a catalyst and increasing the concentration of a reactant are two ways of speeding up a chemical reaction. Describe two more ways.

_____

_____

_____

_____

27. What clues should you look for to tell you that a chemical reaction has occurred?

_____

_____

_____

_____

28. Describe how iodine can tell you if there is starch in a substance.

_____

_____

_____

_____

29. Most organic compounds are made of just four elements. What are they?

_____

_____

_____

_____

Periodic Table of the Elements

1	2	3	4	5	6	7	8	9	10	11	12	13	14	15	16	17	18
hydrogen 1 **H** 1.00																	helium 2 **He** 4.00
lithium 3 **Li** 6.94	beryllium 4 **Be** 9.01											boron 5 **B** 10.81	carbon 6 **C** 12.01	nitrogen 7 **N** 14.01	oxygen 8 **O** 16.00	fluorine 9 **F** 19.00	neon 10 **Ne** 20.18
sodium 11 **Na** 22.99	magnesium 12 **Mg** 24.31											aluminum 13 **Al** 26.98	silicon 14 **Si** 28.09	phosphorus 15 **P** 30.97	sulfur 16 **S** 32.07	chlorine 17 **Cl** 35.45	argon 18 **Ar** 39.95
potassium 19 **K** 39.10	calcium 20 **Ca** 40.08	scandium 21 **Sc** 44.96	titanium 22 **Ti** 47.87	vanadium 23 **V** 50.94	chromium 24 **Cr** 51.97	manganese 25 **Mn** 54.94	iron 26 **Fe** 55.85	cobalt 27 **Co** 58.93	nickel 28 **Ni** 58.69	copper 29 **Cu** 63.55	zinc 30 **Zn** 65.41	gallium 31 **Ga** 69.72	germanium 32 **Ge** 72.64	arsenic 33 **As** 74.92	selenium 34 **Se** 78.96	bromine 35 **Br** 79.90	krypton 36 **Kr** 83.80
rubidium 37 **Rb** 85.47	strontium 38 **Sr** 87.62	yttrium 39 **Y** 88.91	zirconium 40 **Zr** 91.22	niobium 41 **Nb** 92.91	molybdenum 42 **Mo** 95.94	technetium 43 **Tc** 98	ruthenium 44 **Ru** 101.07	rhodium 45 **Rh** 102.91	palladium 46 **Pd** 106.42	silver 47 **Ag** 107.87	cadmium 48 **Cd** 112.41	indium 49 **In** 114.82	tin 50 **Sn** 118.71	antimony 51 **Sb** 121.76	tellurium 52 **Te** 127.60	iodine 53 **I** 126.90	xenon 54 **Xe** 131.29
cesium 55 **Cs** 132.91	barium 56 **Ba** 137.33	lutetium 71 **Lu** 174.97	hafnium 72 **Hf** 178.49	tantalum 73 **Ta** 180.95	tungsten 74 **W** 183.84	rhenium 75 **Re** 186.21	osmium 76 **Os** 190.23	iridium 77 **Ir** 192.22	platinum 78 **Pt** 195.08	gold 79 **Au** 196.97	mercury 80 **Hg** 200.59	thallium 81 **Tl** 204.38	lead 82 **Pb** 207.2	bismuth 83 **Bi** 208.98	polonium 84 **Po** 209	astatine 85 **At** 210	radon 86 **Rn** 222
francium 87 **Fr** 223.00	radium 88 **Ra** 226.00	lawrencium 103 **Lr** 262.00	rutherfordium 104 **Rf** 261.00	dubnium 105 **Db** 262.00	seaborgium 106 **Sg** 266.00	bohrium 107 **Bh** 264.00	hassium 108 **Hs** 269.00	meitnerium 109 **Mt** 268.00	ununnillium 110 **Uun** 271.00	unununium 111 **Uuu** 272.00	ununbium 112 **Uub** 285.00		ununquadium 114 **Uuq** 289.00		ununhexium 116 **Uuh** ???????		ununoctium 118 **Uuo** ???????

lanthanum 57 **La** 138.91	cerium 58 **Ce** 140.12	praseodymium 59 **Pr** 140.91	neodymium 60 **Nd** 144.24	promethium 61 **Pm** 145	samarium 62 **Sm** 150.36	europium 63 **Eu** 151.96	gadolinium 64 **Gd** 157.25	terbium 65 **Tb** 158.93	dysprosium 66 **Dy** 162.50	holmium 67 **Ho** 164.93	erbium 68 **Er** 167.26	thulium 69 **Tm** 168.93	ytterbium 70 **Yb** 173.04
actinium 89 **Ac** 227.00	thorium 90 **Th** 232.04	protactinium 91 **Pa** 231.04	uranium 92 **U** 238.03	neptunium 93 **Np** 237	plutonium 94 **Pu** 244	americium 95 **Am** 243	curium 96 **Cm** 247	berkelium 97 **Bk** 247.00	californium 98 **Cf** 251.00	einsteinium 99 **Es** 252.00	fermium 100 **Fm** 257.00	mendeleevium 101 **Md** 258.00	nobelium 102 **No** 259.00

Assessment Date

Unit 5: Chemistry

Before you retake the Unit Assessment, use the table to figure out which activities you should review.

Question Review Table

Circle the numbers of the questions that you missed on the Unit Assessment. Review the activities that correspond with these questions.

Question	Lesson	Review Activity
1,2	2: The Periodic Table of Elements	Explore: The Periodic Table
3, 5,8,11	1: Atoms and Elements	Explore: Element-ary Science
4,6	2: The Periodic Table of Elements	Explore: The Periodic Table Adopt an Element More Elemental Stuff
7	3: Compounds and Molecules	Explore: Elements Get Together – Chemically Modeling Molecules Surrounded by Compounds
9	4: Chemical Reactions	Explore: Chemical Reactions Reaction!
10	8: Reaction Rates	Explore: Reaction Rates
11,12,13,14	1: Atoms and Elements	Explore: Element-ary Science At the Electron Hotel
15,16	2: The Periodic Table	Explore: The Periodic Table Atomic Calculations Adopt an Element
17,18,19,20,21,22	3: Compounds and Molecules	Explore: Elements Get Together Modeling Molecules
23	3: Compounds and Molecules	Explore: Elements Get Together
24,25	5: Acids and Bases	Explore: Acids and Bases Testing Acids and Bases Cabbage Juice Indicator
26	6: Identification of Compounds	Explore: Identifying Compounds

27	8: Reaction Rates	Explore: Reaction Rates Quick Action Reaction Flour Power-Surface Area and Reactions
28	4: Chemical Reactions	Explore: Chemical Reactions Reaction!
29	6: Identification of Compounds	Start Search
30	7: Molecules of Life	Explore: The Molecules of Our Lives Review Carbohydrates, Proteins, and Lipids Molecular Models

Student Guide
Lesson 1: The Cell Theory

Compared to most scientific discoveries, ideas about cells began forming not that long ago. In the 1600s, people began wondering about what makes up living things. We now know that the smallest part of any living thing is a cell--with organelles that perform jobs much like the organs in your body. Learn the parts of plant and animal cells and their jobs.

All living things are made of cells. Cells are the "building blocks" of living things, from the leaves of a marigold to a duck's webbed feet. You'd think that cells would be tiny--and they usually are. But some cells are large enough for you to see and hold. Learn the cell theory and explore the basic parts of cells.

Lesson Objectives

- Identify the major structures of the cell (such as cell membrane, cytoplasm, and nucleus) and describe their functions.
- Describe the three major ideas of the cell theory.

PREPARE

Approximate lesson time is 60 minutes.

Materials

For the Student

📖 Did You Know?

Keywords and Pronunciation

Anton van Leeuwenhoek (AHN-tohn vahn LAY-ven-hook)

cell : The basic unit of life, of which all living things are made. Some organisms are made up of only one cell.

cell membrane : The flexible, double-layered covering of all cells. The cell membrane is composed of a double layer of molecules.

chloroplast (KLOR-uh-plast) : The "solar panel" of plant cells, in which energy from the sun is converted into stored chemical energy by the process of photosynthesis. Chloroplasts contain chlorophyll and are found in plant cells, but not in animal cells.

cytoplasm (SIY-tuh-pla-zuhm) : The jelly-like matter of a living cell that is outside the nucleus. Organelles are contained in cytoplasm.

endocrine (EN-duh-kruhn)

Francesco Redi (frahn-CHAYS-koh REHD-ee)

Matthias Schleiden (mah-TEE-uhs SHLIY-duhn)

nucleus (NOO-klee-uhs) : The command center of plant and animal cells, which contains the information needed to direct activities for building, maintaining and operating the cell. Information in the nucleus determines which molecules the cell makes.

prokaryotes (proh-KAIR-ee-ohts)

Rudolf Virchow (ROO-dawlf FIHR-koh)

LEARN

Activity 1: What Are You Made Of? *(Online)*

Activity 2: Did You Know? *(Online)*

What's the difference between Hooke and Anton van Leeuwenhoek? Find out through a review of cells and their discovery with an interactive time line.

ASSESS

Lesson Assessment: The Cell Theory (*Online*)

You will complete an offline assessment covering the main objectives of this lesson. Your learning coach will score this assessment.

Name _____   Date _____

Did You Know?

Did you know major cell discoveries have been taking place for hundreds of years? But that's not all! Use the lesson and the links in Lesson Resources to answer the questions and learn lesser-known facts about the development of the cell theory.

1. Did you know people once thought living things could come from nonliving things? What scientist proved this idea wrong by experimenting with rotting meat? _____

2. Did you know the first person to observe cells through a microscope thought they looked like tiny rooms? Who observed these cells?

   _____

3. Did you know the inventor of the simple microscope kept how he made it a secret until he died? What is a simple microscope? Who invented it? _____

   _____

   _____

4. Did you know that scientists once thought the "dark spot" in cells wasn't important? Name the Scottish botanist who paid attention to this spot and named it "nucleus." _____

5. Did you know that the botanist who stated that plants are made of cells started his career as a lawyer? Who was that lawyer-turned-botanist? _____

6. Did you know that it took longer to figure out that animals are also made of cells? Name the botanist who proposed this idea.

   _____

Did You Know?

7. Do you know the first two statements of the cell theory?
   Write them here:

   a. _____

   _____

   b. _____

   _____

8. Did you know the scientist who developed the third part of the cell theory was once challenged to a duel... of sausages? Who was this scientist? _____

9. What is the third statement of the cell theory?

   c. _____

   _____

Did You Know?

Cell Diagram
Draw a diagram of a cell that includes a nucleus, membrane, and cytoplasm.

Name _____   Date _____

Lesson Assessment

Fill in the blanks to complete the cell theory.

1. All _____ are made of cells.
2. The _____ is the basic unit of structure and function in living things.
3. Living cells come only from _____.

4. Draw a cell with a nucleus, cytoplasm, and cell membrane.

A *simile* compares one thing to something else that functions in a similar way. For example, you might say a person who works very hard for a long time is "like a machine." What is a cell like? How about its parts? Choose something to compare a cell and its parts to and explain why you made those choices.

5. A cell is like... _____

_____

Lesson Assessment

6. A nucleus is like… _____

_____

7. Cytoplasm is like… _____

_____

_____

8. A cell membrane is like… _____

_____

Student Guide
Lesson 2: Cell Organelles

Inside cells are parts, called *organelles,* which are responsible for carrying out the cell's life processes. Study cell organelles and their functions and make a model cell that you can eat.

Lesson Objectives

- Recognize the major cell organelles (for example, endoplasmic reticulum, ribosomes, Golgi bodies, chloroplasts, chromosomes, mitochondria, and vacuoles) and describe their functions.
- Distinguish between plant and animal cells.

PREPARE

Approximate lesson time is 60 minutes.

Advance Preparation

- You will need certain foods to make a cell model. These foods are prunes, mandarin oranges, grapes, a carrot, raisins, a tortilla, and a banana.

- Before the lesson, shred the carrot. Cut the shreds so they are small. Tear strips of tortilla and slice thin pieces of banana.

Materials

For the Student

    📖 This Is Your Life, Cell!

    📖 A Cell You Can Eat

    bag, clear plastic (2)

    food - carrot shreds

    food - green grapes

    food - Mandarin oranges

    food - prunes

    food - raisins

    pot with lid

    twist tie (2)

    bowl - large mixing

    gelatin - yellow

    spoon

    water - boiling

Keywords and Pronunciation

cell wall : The stiff structure outside the cell membrane in a plant cell that provides support for the cell. Animal cells do not have cell walls.

chloroplast (KLOR-uh-plast) : The "solar panel" of plant cells, in which energy from the sun is converted into stored chemical energy by the process of photosynthesis. Chloroplasts contain chlorophyll and are found in plant cells, but not in animal cells.

chromosomes (KROH-muh-sohms) : Thread-like structures containing protein and made of DNA, which itself contains the instructions for building, maintaining, and operating the cell.

cytoplasm (SIY-tuh-pla-zuhm) : The jelly-like matter of a living cell that is outside the nucleus. Organelles are contained in cytoplasm.

endoplasmic reticulum (EN-doh-plaz-mihk rih-TIHK-kyuh-luhm) : An organelle that makes, stores, and transports molecules in the cell. Ribosomes are found in some parts of the endoplasmic reticulum.

Golgi (GOHL-jee)

Golgi bodies (GOHL-jee) : Organelles that package molecules to send elsewhere within a cell. Golgi bodies are named for Camillo Golgi, who first described the structures in 1898.

mitochondria (miy-tuh-KAHN-dree-uh) : "Power plants" in the cytoplasm, where energy is released to a usable form, for organisms to function. The singular is mitochondrion. Mitochondria are dense in muscle cells, which need plenty of energy to contract.

organelle (or-guh-NEL) : A differentiated structure within a cell--such as a mitochondrion, vacuole, or chloroplast--that performs a specific function. A mitochondrion is an organelle that changes chemical energy into a form that the cell can use.

ribosomes (RIY-buh-sohmz) : Organelles that produce protein for the cell. Ribosomes build proteins according to instructions from chromosomes.

vacuoles (VA-kyuh-wohls) : Organelles that store food, water, and wastes in a cell and help get rid of wastes. In a plant cell, a large central vacuole takes up most of the cell.

LEARN
Activity 1: Inside a Cell (Online)

Activity 2: This Is Your Life, Cell! (Offline)

If a cell had feelings, it would probably be grateful to all of its organelles for the many jobs they perform. Reunite a happy plant cell with its organelles by identifying the organelles based on their descriptions. Welcome to This Is Your Life, Cell!

Activity 3: A Cell You Can Eat (Offline)

At your next birthday party, why not serve your guests cytoplasm jello and chromosome carrot shreds? Review organelles by making a cell you can eat.

Safety

This lesson involves eating or working with food. Before beginning, check with your doctor, if necessary, to find out whether your student will have any allergic reaction to the food.

ASSESS

Lesson Assessment: Cell Organelles (*Online*)

You will complete an offline assessment covering the main objectives of this lesson. Your learning coach will score this assessment.

LEARN

Activity 4: Visit a Virtual Cell (*Online*)

Explore cells further with a look at a virtual cell. Click the arrow to continue.

<u>Name</u> _____ **Date** _____

This Is Your Life, Cell!

Read the script from This is Your Life, Cell! Fill in the blanks with the names of cell organelles. Use the Word Bank to help you.

Word Bank

Nucleus	Cell Membrane	Mitochondria
Cell Wall	Golgi Body	Vacuole
Chloroplasts	Ribosomes	Cytoplasm
Chromosomes	Endoplasmic Reticulum	

(Lights on, crowd cheers)

BART FRANKLIN, HOST: Welcome, kids, to "This is Your Life" --a show that's guaranteed to bring a smile to your face and a tear to your eye. I'm Bart Franklin, your always-smiling, always-talking host. Today our guest is Cell—a small little guy, but alive and kicking nonetheless. Cell is here to be reunited with his old friends, the organelles. How are you feeling, Cell?

CELL *(in a young voice):* Well, Bart, I can't believe I am here. I am so happy, I could split!

BART: Woah! That's pretty serious, kids! Do you know what happens when cells divide? More cells. We had better get this show started before we've got more than we can handle. But first, let's see whom Cell's brought to the show. Cell?

CELL: Bart, I've brought some of my good friends today-- there's Muscle Cell and Nerve Cell. I also brought Red Blood Cell, but he doesn't talk much on account of the fact that he doesn't have a nucleus.

BART: Well, that is a shame, Cell. Speaking of nucleus, would you believe we've got your pal Nucleus right here in the studio tonight?

This Is Your Life, Cell!

CELL: No! Not old Nucleus!

BART: It's true. Now, before we've got double trouble on our hands, how about we begin?

CELL: Sure thing, Bart!

BART: Okay, Cell. Listen to this first mystery guest.

GUEST 1 *(in a rubbery, shaky voice):* Hi ya, Cell. I'm the guy that holds it all together for ya. I hold your nucleus, your chloroplasts, even your endoplasmic reticulum. I'm kinda jelly-like. Once, I helped you stretch out and sorta change shape because I give ya your shape. Do you remember me?

CELL *(thinking):* Hmmm… Jelly-like? Holds all my organelles? You must be _____ !

BART: Excellent work. *(crowd claps)* Let's hear from mystery guest number two.

GUEST 2 *(in a hurried voice):* Oh, Cell, Cell, I could hardly come today--I was so busy changing chemical energy into something you can use. I am always changing energy, like changing a check into money at the bank. Tell me quickly who I am so I can get back to work.

CELL *(excited):* Oh, I remember you! You were always a powerhouse! You're _____!

BART: Two for two! *(crowd claps)* Okay, Cell, see if you can figure out this third mystery guest…

This Is Your Life, Cell!

GUEST 3 *(in an intelligent voice):* Ah, yes, Cell. Long time, no diffusion. Well, in order for you to do your job, you need me to give you instructions. I have all of the genetic information in me inside a long molecule called DNA. Just who might I be?

CELL: Is that you, Nucleus?

BART: Ooooooh, Cell, not this time. *(crowd gasps)* But I hang out with Nucleus. Try again. Think DNA and genetic information.

CELL *(with a smile):* It can't be…I thought you'd been copied long ago. Is it _____?

BART: Thatta boy, Cell! *(crowd claps)* Be sure to save a hug for your old pal. *(crowd sighs)* Okay, Cell. Now things are going to get a little tough. We've got two organelles here this time because they are often found together. Listen closely to the next mystery guests!

GUEST 4 *(a tiny voice):* Cell, it is so good to see you. Just backstage I was talking to Chromosomes and we were remembering how I used to follow their instructions to put together proteins. You often find me in the folds of the next mystery guest.

GUEST 5 *(a deep voice from offstage):* Cell…some have described my looks as a maze, but you can't get lost in me. I let my buddy here stay within my membrane network. I also store and move molecules. I hope you know who I am, Cell, because it's been a long time and I sure miss ya.

CELL: Wow, this is a tough one, Bart. There's only one maze-like network I know that lets molecules in and out. It's _____ _____. And that fourth guest that can be found there… that must be _____!

This Is Your Life, Cell!

BART: Excellent job, Cell! Just look at the crowd cheering! *(clapping)* Since you did so well with two organelles last time, let's try that again. Plus, we're running out of time and we've got to show some commercials before our next guest, Mr. Zinc. He's getting quite unstable backstage. Let's hear from our next two mystery guests.

GUEST 6 *(a kind voice):* Cell! The flight here was terrible! I felt sick, but no one could tell because I am already green. Remember all those times you were hungry? I was able to take the sun's energy and change it into chemical energy so you were fed. It was not an easy job, but I was happy to do it for you all these years.

GUEST 7 *(a tough voice):* Cell, I've got some bumps and bruises and my back hurts from holding you up so rigidly for so long. I gave you your shape, remember? My feet hurt a little, too. Many times I thought about quitting, but I am loyal to you, Cell.

CELL *(about to cry):* Bart, I'd know those two anywhere. They are the reason I am a plant cell. Come on out here, _____ and _____!

BART: Aw, gee folks, isn't that sweet? Cell, we just got great news. One of your organelles was not able to make it today, but we've got her on the phone. Listen in carefully to this guest!

GUEST 8 *(a military voice):* Hello there, Cell! Hold on a second there--*(away from the phone)* hey molecules--get over here, please! It's time to package you up and send you to other areas. Quit moving around now, you've got a job to do! *(back on phone)* I'm sorry, Cell, there's a lot to do around here. Do you know who I am?

CELL: Is that you, Vacuole?

This Is Your Life, Cell!

GUEST 8: Do I sound like a liquid bubble? I do a hard job for you Cell, packaging up molecules and sending them on their way. Try again!

CELL: Could it be you, _____?

BART: Cell! You've done it again. *(crowd cheers)* Okay, just two more to go. Next guest!

GUEST 9 *(with a British accent):* Hallo there, Cell! It's me, back here directing everyone else. Mitochondria, I do wish you would stay still. Goodness chromosomes, what *are* you doing? Very well. Cell, you know me. I direct all of your activities, like a command center inside you.

CELL: It's _____! How are you? Don't work too hard back there!

BART: He's done it again! Okay, Cell, we've got one more organelle here to see you today. Let's listen in and see if you can identify this last mystery guest.

GUEST 10 *(a motherly voice):* Oh Cell, Cell, Cell…without me, you'd have no shape. I protect you like a skin. I am the outermost layer of you, next to the wall. Remember when we looked like a rectangle, then sort of like a rounded rectangle? That was Cytoplasm and me! I also let things pass into and out of you. Do you remember me?

CELL *(in tears)*: Could it be? I know that voice anywhere… Is that you, _____?

BART: You've done it! *(crowd cheers and claps)* Excellent, Cell. In just a moment we'll reunite you with all your cell organelles-- except Golgi Body, of course. She wishes she could have been here today.

This Is Your Life, Cell!

CELL: I can hardly wait.

BART: That's great, Cell. Before we go, have you got anything you'd like to say?

CELL: This has been amazing, Bart. When do I get to take my trip to Hawaii?

BART: Well, this isn't that kind of show, Cell. But we *can* reunite you with your organelles-- how about it, folks?

CELL: But I'd rather go to Hawaii!

BART: Cell, you'e kind of rooted here. You live in an evergreen tree. I just don't think Hawaii is possible. But we have some nice parting gifts, including the board game version of "This is Your Life!" How about we get all your organelles out here for a great big hug--come on, gang! We need to cut to a commercial, be right back!

CELL: But I learned to hula!

(lights go down)

Name _____ Date _____

A Cell You Can Eat

Why do scientists make models? Models help us study things we can't easily see.

You can make a model of a cell using different fruits to represent different organelles. Study the chart. Fill in either the name of the cell organelle or its description. When you finish, make a cell you can eat!

Fruit	Cell Organelle	Description
Prune		Command center, directs cell activities
Gelatin	Cytoplasm	
Mandarin oranges		Change chemical energy to a form that is usable by the cell
Green grapes	Chloroplasts	
Carrot shreds		Contains the genetic information for the cell in its DNA
Raisins	Ribosome	
Thin pieces of tortilla, stacked and crumpled		A maze-like network of membranes that store or move molecules in the cell
Thin slices of banana, stacked		Packages molecules to send to other places in the cell
Bag	Cell membrane	
Cup		Rigid, gives plant cells their shape

Name _____   Date _____

A Cell You Can Eat

Make the Model

Materials

2 plastic sandwich bags   carrot shreds
twist ties   raisins
boiling water   thin strips of tortilla, folded
large mixing bowls   thin slices of banana, stacked
spoons   cup (8 oz)
prune   water
gelatin, yellow   heat source
Mandarin oranges   pot
green grapes

Procedure

1. Leave one plastic bag open. This represents the cell membrane of an animal cell.
2. Place the second bag into the cup, completely lining the cup with a little extra sticking out from the top. This represents the cell membrane and cell wall of a plant cell.
3. Make gelatin following the directions on the packet.
4. Place the cell bag close to full with warm gelatin. This represents the cytoplasm.
5. Place the cell "organelles" into the bag: a prune to represent a nucleus with a few carrot shred chromosomes stuck inside, mandarin oranges for mitochondria, several bananna slices stacked together for a golgi body, folded tortilla strips for endoplasmic reticulum, and raisins for ribosomes. Place a few "ribosomes" between the layers of "endoplasmic reticulum."
6. Close the "cell" using the twist tie.
7. Repeat steps 5 and 6 for the plant cell, adding grapes for chloroplasts.
8. Put them in the refrigerator to set.

Name _____   Date _____

A Cell You Can Eat

Questions

1. What parts do plant and animal cells have in common? List all of them, not just those used in the model. _____

   _____

   _____

2. What parts are different between plant and animal cells? How does this affect what the cells do? _____

   _____

   _____

   _____

3. If you were looking at cells with a microscope, how would you know whether they came from a plant or an animal? _____

   _____

   _____

4. What types of cells have chloroplasts? What function do chloroplasts serve? _____

   _____

5. What information do chromosomes carry? _____

   _____

   _____

Name _____   Date _____

Lesson Assessment

Choose the best answer.

1. Which organelle changes chemical energy into a form that is usable by the cell?
   A. mitochondria
   B. ribosome
   C. nucleus
   D. cell wall

2. Which organelle holds genetic information in the molecule DNA?
   A. vacuole
   B. cell membrane
   C. chromosome
   D. Golgi body

3. Which tiny, round "factory" puts together protein and is often found in the endoplasmic reticulum?
   A. chromosome
   B. chloroplast
   C. Golgi body
   D. ribosome

4. Which organelle is responsible for packaging molecules to send to other places in the cell?
   A. mitochondria
   B. vacuole
   C. Golgi body
   D. nucleus

5. Which organelle appears to be empty but is filled with liquid?
   A. cell membrane
   B. chloroplast
   C. vacuole
   D. ribosome

Lesson Assessment

6. Study the illustration. Which cell is likely to come from a plant?

A.   B.

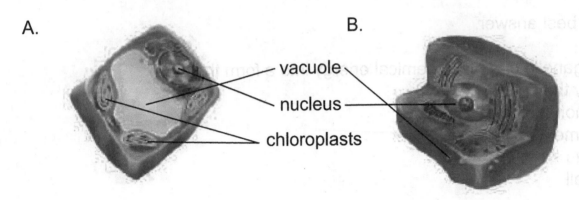

vacuole

nucleus

chloroplasts

7. How is a cell membrane different from a cell wall? _____

_____

_____

_____

_____

8. What parts are different between plant and animal cells? How does this affect what the cells can do? _____

_____

_____

_____

_____

Student Guide
Lesson 3: Diffusion, Osmosis, and Active Transport

And now, more activities from those busy cells! The movement of molecules is one of a cell's basic processes. How else could it be fed, pass nerve signals, or secrete hormones when they are needed? Explore diffusion, osmosis, and active transport: three ways cells are able to get particles in and out through their cell membranes. Make models to observe diffusion through a plastic "membrane" and osmosis through the cell membrane of an egg.

Lesson Objectives

- Recognize various ways in which molecules are transported across the cell membrane.
- Define *diffusion* as the process by which molecules move from areas of higher concentration to areas of lower concentration.
- Recognize that water moves through membranes by *osmosis*--diffusion of water through a semipermeable membrane.

PREPARE

Approximate lesson time is 60 minutes.

Advance Preparation

- The model cells you make in this lesson will need to stand overnight. You may start the lesson and come back to it the next day or prepare this activity ahead of time. Print the Diffusion Through a Membrane activity sheet for directions.
- Follow the directions in the Osmosis activity sheet to soak an egg in vinegar for at least two days. If, after two days, the shell is not completely dissolved or softened, leave the egg in vinegar an extra day.

Materials

For the Student

📖 Diffusion Through a Membrane

bag, clear plastic - sandwich bags-no zipper

cornstarch - 5 mL (1 tsp)

drinking glass - 355 mL (12oz) (2)

iodine

measuring spoon - teaspoon

rock - small

eyedropper

graduated cylinder

measuring cup

spoon - mixing

string - 30 cm (2)

water

📖 Osmosis

food - corn syrup

food - one raw egg

household item - clear 500 mL containers (2)

vinegar - 250 mL

graduated cylinder - 250 mL

spoon

tape - masking

Keywords and Pronunciation

cell membrane : The flexible, double-layered covering of cells. Cell membranes help control what goes in and out of cells.

cytoplasm (SIY-tuh-pla-zuhm) : The jelly-like matter of a living cell that is outside the nucleus. Organelles are contained in cytoplasm.

diffusion : The process by which molecules tend to move from an area of higher concentration to an area of lower concentration. Diffusion of molecules from onions frying in the kitchen brings the smell to the living room.

osmosis (ahz-MOH-suhs) : the diffusion of water across a semipermeable membrane

permeable (PUHR-mee-uh-buhl) : Allowing molecules to pass or diffuse through. Any barrier or membrane that lets molecules through it is said to be permeable to those molecules.

semipermeable : Permeable to some molecules, but not to others. Cell membranes are semipermeable, permeable to water molecules, but not to larger molecules.

turgor (TUHR-guhr) : outward force on the cell wall of a plant that results from water contained within the cell; turgid pressure helps keep a plant rigid.

LEARN
Activity 1: Moving Through Membranes *(Online)*

Activity 2: Diffusion Through a Membrane *(Offline)*

Not all barriers are molecule proof! In cells, diffusion involves molecules passing through a cell "barrier," or membrane, as well as from one place to another where no membrane exists. Observe the diffusion of iodine molecules using a model system.

Safety

Use caution when using a heat source and handling boiling water. Never leave your student unattended near boiling water.

Activity 3: Osmosis *(Offline)*

Sadly, putting a book under your pillow won't help you learn by osmosis. But you can observe how osmosis happens in other parts of your body--namely your cells.

ASSESS

Lesson Assessment: Diffusion, Osmosis, and Active Transport *(Online)*

You will complete an online assessment covering the main objectives of this lesson. Your assessment will be scored by the computer.

Name _____ Date _____

Diffusion Through a Membrane

Diffusion takes place when molecules in a gas or liquid spread out, moving from a place where they are highly concentrated to a place where they are not as concentrated. You experience the result of diffusion when smells from a kitchen reach you in a far-away room. Where is the area of high concentration of smelly molecules? _____ Where is the area of low concentration of smelly molecules? _____

_____

Diffusion also happens in cells as molecules move in and out through the cell membrane. You can make a model to see how this works.

Materials
water
plastic sandwich bag (not the zipper-close type), 2
cornstarch
iodine
cup, 355 mL (12 oz.), 2
graduated cylinder
measuring spoon
measuring cup
small rock
marker

Procedure
1. Fill both bags with 5 mL cornstarch and 120 mL water.
2. Add a small rock about the size of a golf ball to each bag.
3. Knot the top of the bags to close them.
4. Fill the cups halfway with water.
5. Add 10 drops of iodine to one of the cups. Label this Cup 1. The cup of plain water will be Cup 2.
6. Place the bags in the cup. Completely submerge the bag of cornstarch mixture.

Diffusion Through a Membrane

7. Wait 15 minutes, then make your observations. While waiting, answer the questions.

Questions
Think about concentrations. A more concentrated substance has more "stuff" in a given amount of it. A less concentrated substance has less "stuff."

1. In which is starch more concentrated—the bag or the cup?

_____

2. For Cup 1: In which is iodine more concentrated—the bag or the cup? _____

	Starting Color	Color after 15 minutes
Solution in Cup 1		
Bag in Cup 1		
Solution in Cup 2		
Bag in Cup 2		

Analysis
You know that iodine changes to a deep purple-black when it comes into contact with starch. Use your observations to answer the questions.

1. Which substance moved, the iodine or the starch? _____

2. How can you tell? _____

_____

_____

_____

_____

Diffusion Through a Membrane

3. The plastic bag allowed which molecules to pass through— water, cornstarch, or iodine? _____

4. Diffusion happens when molecules move from areas of high concentration to areas of low concentration. Which substance diffused? _____

5. What was the purpose of Cup 2? _____

6. Sketch Cup 1 and its bag below. Label the areas of high concentration and low concentration at the start for both starch and iodine. Use arrows to show how diffusion happened in this investigation.

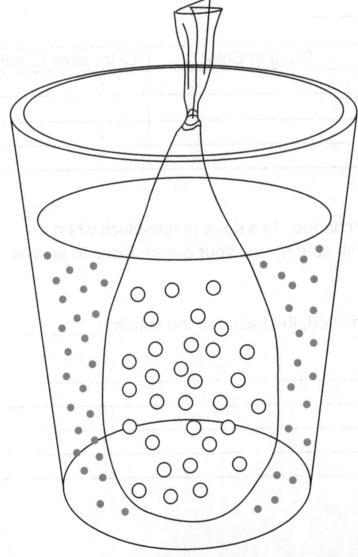

Diffusion Through a Membrane

Conclusion

1. Explain how diffusion occurred in this investigation. Use your observations to write a detailed answer. _____

_____

_____

_____

_____

_____

_____

2. What would happen if you did this experiment again, but placed iodine in the bag and the cornstarch solution in the cup?

_____

_____

3. Tell why it is not a good idea to store iodine in a plastic bag.

_____

_____

_____

Name _____   Date _____

Osmosis

A membrane that is *semipermeable* will let some things through, but not others. If water molecules are able to pass from a high-concentration area to a low-concentration area through membranes like this, we call it *osmosis*.

A key fact to remember about osmosis is that it involves the movement of water molecules. Diffusion involves liquid and gas molecules, but when you are thinking about osmosis, think about water.

Use an egg to see how osmosis works.

Materials
one raw egg
two clear 500 mL containers
plates, 2
250 mL vinegar
250 mL corn syrup
water
spoon
masking tape
marker
graduated cylinder
measuring cups

Procedure:
1. Use the masking tape and marker to label the containers A and B.
2. Pour 250 mL of vinegar into container A. Mark the level of the vinegar with a piece of masking tape.
3. Pour 250 mL of syrup into container B. Compare the levels of the liquids in containers A and B to make sure they are the same. Mark the level of the syrup with a piece of masking tape.
4. Place the egg into container A. Make sure it is completely covered. Cover both containers with plates or other lids.
5. After two days, use the spoon to very carefully remove the egg from container A. Rinse the egg and place it into container B.
6. Mark the new level of the vinegar in container A with masking tape.

<u>Name</u> _____   <u>Date</u> _____

Osmosis

7. Observe the egg the next day. Record its appearance in the Observations section on page 2.

8. Remove the egg and place it in water. Mark the new level of the syrup in container B with masking tape.

Observations

After two days in vinegar, what is the appearance of the egg? _____

_____

After another day in the syrup, what is the appearance of the egg?_____

_____

Was there more or less vinegar in container A after two days? _____

Was there more or less syrup in container B after one day? _____

Analysis

Follow directions *carefully* to answer the questions.

1. In container A, how can you tell that water from the vinegar moved into the egg? _____

_____

_____

2. In container B, how can you tell that water moved out of the egg?

_____

_____

3. The egg has many molecules in its cytoplasm, some of which are water. Why did water move into the egg in container A? Tell about the concentrations of water molecules._____

_____

_____

_____

Osmosis

4. Why did water move out of the egg in container B? Tell about the concentrations of water molecules. _____

_____

_____

Conclusions

1. What part of the egg controlled what moved into and out of the egg? _____

2. What would happen if you left the egg you removed from the syrup in water? Explain your answer. _____

_____

_____

Student Guide
Lesson 4: Photosynthesis and Respiration

All the energy that living organisms use begins with the sun. Without the sun, plants would not be able to make their own food. Without food, plants would die. And without plants, animals--including humans--would not survive. Study the processes of photosynthesis and respiration, which are the keys to the flow of energy in life. Investigate the process of photosynthesis using a common household plant.

Lesson Objectives

- Describe the process of *cellular respiration*.
- Describe the process of *photosynthesis* in plants.

PREPARE

Approximate lesson time is 60 minutes.

Advance Preparation

- Find a houseplant and a sunny location. Print Where are the Stomata? and follow the directions to set up the investigation. Coat the top sides of four leaves with a heavy layer of petroleum jelly. Coat the undersides of four other leaves with petroleum jelly. Place the plant in normal sunlight and water as usual for one week. Observe the plant during the lesson.
- You will need a sprig of elodea if you choose to do the Beyond the Lesson activity. You can buy elodea at a pet store or any other store that sells fish supplies.

Materials

For the Student

🖥 Yes, Teacher!

🖥 A Lot of Stomata

  petroleum jelly

  plant - with broad leaves

  knife - butter

🖥 Exhale!

  food - purple cabbage, head

  household item - drinking straw

  household item - heat source

  jar - pint size-with lids (3)

  plant - sprig of elodea

  aluminum foil

  bowl - mixing

  water

  water - distilled

Keywords and Pronunciation

chlorophyll (KLOR-uh-fil) : A special, large molecule that "captures" light energy and starts its change into chemical energy in the process of photosynthesis. Chlorophyll gives many plants their green color.

chloroplasts (KLOR-uh-plasts) : Structures in green plant cells that enable plants to produce their own food by converting light energy into chemical energy in molecules of glucose. Animal cells do not have chloroplasts.

mitochondria (miy-tuh-KAHN-dree-uh) : "Power plants" in the cytoplasm, where energy is released to a usable form, for organisms to function. The singular is mitochondrion. Mitochondria are dense in muscle cells, which need plenty of energy to contract.

photosynthesis (foh-toh-SINT-thuh-suhs) : The process by which plant cells convert light energy from the sun into chemical energy. During photosynthesis, plants use the sun´s energy to make glucose out of carbon dioxide and water, releasing oxygen. Photosynthesis means "putting together with light."

respiration : The process by which most living things convert the chemical energy in glucose into more accessible chemical energy in ATP. During respiration, cells break down glucose into carbon dioxide and water, using oxygen in the process. The overall process of cellular respiration is the reverse of photosynthesis.

stomata (STOH-muh-tuh) : Microscopic openings in the leaves of plants through which the plant takes in and releases gases. Stomata are found on the undersides of leaves.

LEARN

Activity 1: Energy Flows *(Online)*

Activity 2: Photosynthesis and Respiration Review *(Offline)*

Photosynthesis means "putting together with light." Now you will put together information using a pencil. Review photosynthesis and respiration.

Activity 3: Gas Exchange in Plants *(Offline)*

A photosynthesis "recipe" requires several ingredients: some carbon dioxide and water, a little sunlight, and a chemical reaction. What happens when a plant can't get all the ingredients it needs? See what happens when a change affects a plant's ability to "cook" its own food.

ASSESS

Lesson Assessment: Photosynthesis and Respiration *(Online)*

You will complete an offline assessment covering the main objectives of this lesson. Your learning coach will score this assessment.

LEARN
Activity 4: Exhale! *(Offline)*

Did you know that plants as well as animals exhale carbon dioxide? During the day, plants use sunlight for photosynthesis. What happens at night when there's no sun? Test for the presence of carbon dioxide using a cabbage-juice indicator.

Safety

When using the drinking straw in the Beyond the Lesson activity, exhale only. Do not inhale or drink the indicator.

Name _____   Date _____

Yes, Teacher!

Imagine you are responsible for teaching someone about photosynthesis and cellular respiration. Follow the directions to help prepare these notes and diagrams for your student. Afterward, make a colorful poster to help you teach your lesson.

Taking Notes

Start with the basics. Provide your students with a few notes about photosynthesis and respiration. Write the chemical equations for both processes below. Use the Word Bank to help you.

Word Bank

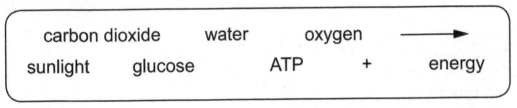

carbon dioxide   water   oxygen   ⟶

sunlight   glucose   ATP   +   energy

Photosynthesis:

_____

Respiration:

_____

Yes, Teacher!

Comparing

Once your students are familiar with photosynthesis and respiration, they should compare them. Comparing is a good way to see how things are either alike or different. Fill out the table to prepare for teaching your students how to compare photosynthesis and respiration.

	Where?	When?	Reactants?	Products?	Energy source?	Energy result?
Photo-synthesis	In cells that have chlorophyll		Carbon dioxide, water			Energy is stored in glucose
Respiration		All the time		Carbon dioxide, water	energy in glucose	

Yes, Teacher!

Drawing a Diagram

Every student learns in a different way. Some may need to see a "picture" or diagram of a process before they understand it completely. Help prepare a diagram for your students.

The diagram below compares photosynthesis and respiration. Fill in the blanks in the diagram to complete the comparison.

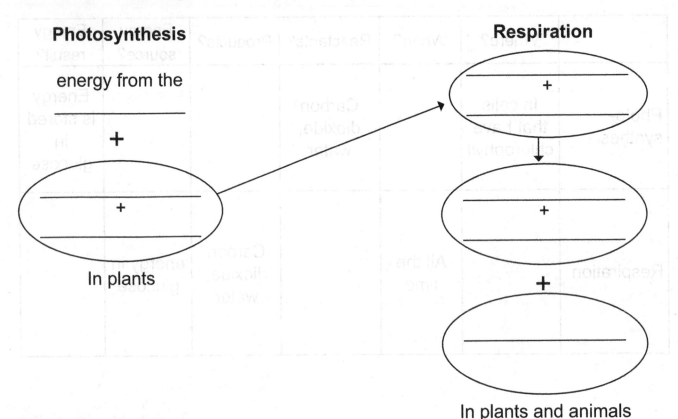

Teach Your Lesson

Use the answer key to check your answers in the Taking Notes, Comparing, and Drawing a Diagram sections. Next, make a poster to teach what you know about photosynthesis and respiration. Your poster should:

- Tell which processes happen in plants and which happen in animals
- List the products and reactants in both
- Explain where the energy comes from or goes to for both
- Use colors and pictures to explain what you are teaching

Share your poster with an adult. Use your poster to teach what you've learned about photosynthesis and respiration. Answer any questions the adult has after your lesson.

Name _____   Date _____

A Lot of Stomata

Fill in the blanks to review gas exchanges in plants during photosynthesis.

_____ and _____ are the gases involved in photosynthesis. During photosynthesis, plants give off _____, and take in _____. What would happen if these gases could not be exchanged in plants?

Suppose you saw microscopic structures that looked like openings on the bottoms of plant leaves, but not on the tops. You wanted to know whether these structures were important in gas exchange for photosynthesis. You could use petroleum jelly to block the openings from taking in and giving off gases. Make a hypothesis that you can test in this experiment, using petroleum jelly to block the openings.

Hypothesis
Predict what will happen to the plant leaves if you coat the bottoms of a few leaves with petroleum jelly. _____

_____

Predict what will happen if you coat the tops of some leaves.

_____

_____

Materials
potted plant
petroleum jelly
butter knife

Procedure
1. Coat the top of two leaves with a heavy layer of petroleum jelly.
2. Coat the undersides of two other leaves with a heavy layer of petroleum jelly.
3. Place the plant in an area where it will receive sunlight. Water the plant as normal.
4. Observe the leaves daily for 1 week.

Name _____   Date _____

A Lot of Stomata

Analysis

1. Which leaves were able to function well during the week? How could you tell? _____

   _____

   _____

2. Which leaves were not able to function well during the week? How could you tell? _____

   _____

   _____

3. What does this tell you about gas exchange and the tiny openings on the bottoms of plant leaves? _____

   _____

   _____

Conclusion

Tiny openings in plant leaves allow gases to move in and out. When the openings are blocked, the plant cannot receive carbon dioxide gas or give off oxygen, so it cannot photosynthesize. Those tiny openings are called *stomata*. Based on your investigation, how are stomata important? _____

_____

_____

_____

_____

Name _____ Date _____

Lesson Assessment

Word Bank

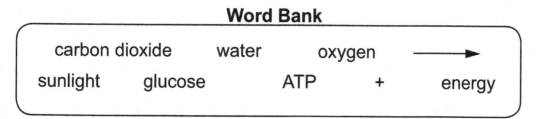

| carbon dioxide | water | oxygen | ⟶ |
| sunlight | glucose | ATP | + | energy |

1. Describe the process of photosynthesis. You may write an equation, draw a picture, or write an explanation. List all of the products and reactants. Explain whether this process takes place in animals, plants, or both. Use the word bank to help you.

_____

_____

_____

2. Describe the process of respiration. You may write an equation, draw a picture, or write an explanation. List all of the products and reactants. Explain whether this process takes place in animals, plants, or both. Use the word bank to help you.

_____

_____

_____

Name _____   Date _____

Exhale!

You now know that photosynthesis involves energy from sunlight. But what happens when the sun goes down? In the dark, plants can use oxygen and food the way animals do. They produce carbon dioxide. You can test for carbon dioxide with a cabbage juice indicator.

The cabbage juice indicator has a dye that turns red when mixed with any acid. Carbon dioxide combines with water to form a weak acid called *carbonic acid*. If the indicator turns red, you will know that carbon dioxide is present.

Materials
distilled water
sprig of elodea
3 pint jars with lids
straw
aluminum foil
head of purple cabbage
water
heat source
mixing bowl

Lab Safety: When using the straw, exhale only. Do not inhale or drink the indicator.

Procedure
Make the Indicator
1. Cut the cabbage into small pieces. You may pull the leaves off and tear them.
2. Place the cabbage pieces into a 2-liter bowl.
3. Heat the distilled water. Add enough to fill the bowl.
4. Let the cabbage stand until the water cools.

Exhale!

5. Strain the liquid. Throw away the cabbage pieces and keep the blue liquid.

Use the Indicator
6. Rinse the jars with distilled water. Label them 1, 2, and 3.
7. Fill all three jars with equal amounts of cabbage juice.
8. Place an elodea plant in Jar 1. Seal the lid tightly and place it in bright sunlight.
9. Place an elodea plant in Jar 2. Close the lid tightly and cover the jar with aluminum foil. Place the jar in a location where it will not be disturbed.
10. Seal Jar 3 and place it in bright light.
11. After two days, observe the color changes in the jars.

Observations
1. Which jars showed a color change? _____
2. Use a straw to EXHALE into the cabbage juice in Jar 3 until a color change occurs. *Do not inhale or drink the cabbage juice.* What substance is added to the cabbage juice as you exhale?

_____

Conclusion
1. What can you conclude about the presence of carbon dioxide in the jars? Do plants give off carbon dioxide? Under what conditions? _____

_____

_____

2. In what process do plants give off carbon dixoide, which occurred in the dark? _____
3. What process occurs in green plants in the light?

_____

4. Why didn't the elodea in the light give off carbon dixoide and change the color of the indicator? _____

_____

_____

Student Guide
Lesson 5. Optional: The Cell Cycle

This lesson is OPTIONAL. It's provided for enrichment or extra practice, but not required for completion of this unit. You may skip this lesson.

Lesson Objectives

- Identify and describe the four stages of mitosis: prophase, metaphase, anaphase, and telophase.
- Recognize that dividing plant and animal cells have a cycle with three phases: interphase, mitosis, and cytokinesis.
- Recognize that *interphase* is a period of growth and the copying of the genetic material.
- Recognize that *mitosis* is a period of division of the cell nucleus.
- Recognize that *cytokinesis* is a final event of cell division after mitosis.
- Demonstrate mastery of the skills taught in this lesson.

PREPARE

Approximate lesson time is 60 minutes.

Advance Preparation

- Wrap two forks, two spoons, and two knives in aluminum foil. They should still resemble forks, spoons, and knives.

Materials

For the Student

　　🖳 Time to Divide

　　　　bags, paper grocery

　　　　rubber band - several

　　　　aluminum foil

　　　　fork - plastic or metal (4)

　　　　knife - plastic or metal-dull (4)

　　　　spoon - plastic or metal (4)

　　　　string

　　　　yarn - different colors (2)

Keywords and Pronunciation

chromosomes (KROH-muh-sohms) : Thread-like structures made of protein and DNA that contain the instructions for building, maintaining, and operating the cell. When a cell is ready for mitosis, its chromosomes begin to condense into thicker structures.

cytokinesis (siy-toh-kuh-NEE-suhs) : The process by which cells complete their division into new cells. Cytokinesis follows the end of mitosis in the cell cycle.

deoxyribonucleic (dee-AHK-sih-riy-boh-nyoo-clay-ick)

DNA : Deoxyribonucleic acid, the molecule carrying the genetic information found in every cell and unique to each individual. All the information an organism needs to live and reproduce is contained in its DNA.

---

mitosis (miy-TOH-suhs) : The process by which cell nuclei divide, separating the genetic material into two complete sets for the new cells. Mitosis follows a period of growth called interphase.

telophase (TEH-luh-fayz)

LEARN

Activity 1. Optional: A Cell's Busy Life (Online)

Cells are always dying, but they are also constantly replacing themselves. They do this through a cycle of growth and genetic material copying, division of the nucleus, and final dividing, in which one cell becomes two. Learn the phases of the cell cycle as well as the stages of mitosis, through which the nucleus divides. Understand the steps in these processes more clearly by using a cell division model.

Activity 2. Optional: Time to Divide: More About the Cell Cycle (Offline)

Another model--this time of the cell cycle! Investigate how one cell becomes two in a fascinating process of replication and division.

Safety

Use dull butter knives or plastic knives, and supervise your student while she is using the knives.

Activity 3. Optional: How Does a Cut Heal? (Online)

How does a cut heal? Learn the role that cells play in fighting infections. See how cell division results in healing cuts. Once you know what goes on underneath, you'll never want to pick off a scab again! Click the arrow to continue.

Safety

You may wish to preview any websites listed in this lesson.

Name _____   Date _____

Time to Divide

Mitosis is the event in a cell's life when its nucleus divides. Place a check below next to the things you already know about mitosis. If there is something you do not know, go back and read the Explore again.

- Cells are always dying and new cells are always being formed.
- Cells contain genetic information in chromosomes.
- Every time a cell is preparing to divide, each chromosome makes an identical copy of itself.
- A new cell has the same exact genetic information as its "parent" cell.

Some things to think about:
- Do all cells of one organism look like one another?
- Do all cells of one organism have the same genetic information?
- How long does it take for one parent cell to become two "daughter" cells?

Study mitosis with a model cell. Imagine this is a body cell from an organism whose chromosomes look like forks, knives, and spoons. Follow the directions to model mitosis.

Make the Cell
1. Use one large piece of paper for your cell. Choose one color of yarn to be the cell membrane and another to be the nuclear membrane, which surrounds the nucleus.

2. Add six chromosomes to the cell: a wrapped fork, spoon, and knife and a plain fork, spoon and knife. Arrange the cell, membranes, and chromosomes on the floor as shown.

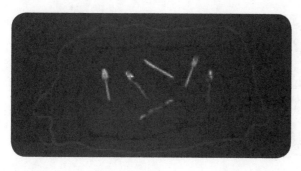

Time to Divide

Interphase

During interphase, chromosomes are stretched out long and stringy and are copied. Imagine the chromosomes in your cell model are stretched out long and stringy.

1. Copy each chromosome by finding six more utensils exactly like the ones already in the nucleus.
2. With a rubber band, attach a wrapped fork to the wrapped fork, a plain fork to the plain fork, and so on. Imagine they are lengthened. Each pair of forks, spoons, and knives connected by a rubber band is one chromosome with two identical copies of its genetic material.

Prophase

During prophase, the copied chromosomes become shorter and the nuclear membrane disappears. Imagine the chromosomes in your model shorten.

- The amount of DNA in a chromosome that copied its genetic material is _____ the amount of DNA in a chromosome that did not copy its genetic material. (half, double, three times)
- The copies of genetic information in each chromosome are _____. (the same, different, empty)

3. Remove the nuclear membrane from around the chromosomes.

Metaphase

During metaphase, the nuclear membrane is gone. Chromosomes line up along the middle of the cell.

4. Add "stringy molecules" stretched across the center of the cell.
5. Arrange the chromosomes in the center of the cell on the stringy molecules. The order does not matter and it is okay if the chromosomes are right-side up or upside down.

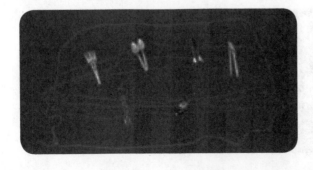

Time to Divide

Anaphase

During anaphase, the stringy molecules pull each chromosome apart. The copies of genetic material separate and move toward the ends of the cell.

6. Separate your original chromosomes to form daughter chromosomes.

7. Move the chromosomes to the outer edge of the cell. Real chromosomes are flexible and bend in the middle as they are dragged through the cytoplasm. Imagine that your chromosomes bend as they are pulled apart.

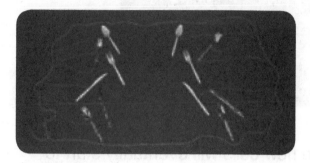

- Are the two sets of daughter chromosomes identical or different?
  _____

- Are the two sets of daughter chromosomes the same as those that were in the parent cell before they copied their genetic material? _____

Telophase

During telophase, the chromosomes stretch out again and two new nuclei are formed. Imagine your cell's chromosomes begin to stretch out again to become long and stringy.

8. Remove the stringy molecules from the chromosomes.

9. Cut the nuclear membrane string to create two new small nuclear membranes in the cell.

10. Start to pinch in the yarn that represents the cell membrane.

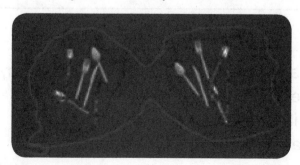

Time to Divide

Cytokinesis

During this phase, one cell finishes becoming two. In animal cells, the cell membrane finishes pinching off. In plant cells, a new cell wall and membrane finish forming.

11. Divide your cell in half. Replace the long string representing the cell membrane with two shorter pieces of the same color representing new membranes of two new cells.

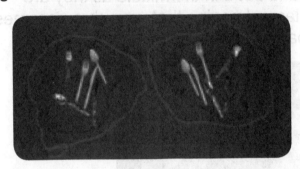

What Next?

The chromosomes in the two new cells will eventually start to copy themselves.

- What phase is this? _____

- Does the parent cell still exist? _____
  _____

- How are the new cells related to each other? _____
  _____
  _____

- What was accomplished by mitosis? _____
  _____
  _____

Practice

You should realize that you can repeat this process over and over, just as cells continue to divide over and over again. Repeat the process, this time explaining it to someone else. Become familiar with the stages so that you can describe them when asked.

Student Guide
Lesson 6. Optional: DNA

This lesson is OPTIONAL. It's provided for enrichment or extra practice, but not required for completion of this unit. You may skip this lesson.

Lesson Objectives

- Describe the structure of DNA as two twisted chains of molecular pieces with pairs of bases attached between them like rungs on a ladder.
- Explain that all the information an organism needs to live and reproduce is contained in its DNA.

PREPARE

Approximate lesson time is 60 minutes.

Advance Preparation

- To make a model of DNA, you will need black and red licorice sticks and either gumdrops, jelly beans, or marshmallows in colors close to red, blue, green, and white. Licorice ropes will work as well. If you use licorice ropes, you will not need to sew the licorice together.
- In addition to the common household items needed to extract DNA, you will need split peas and an enzyme such as meat tenderizer. If you do not have meat tenderizer, try pineapple juice or contact lens cleaning solution.

Materials

For the Student

📖 Treat Yourself to DNA

food - gumdrops or jelly beans

household item - crayons

household item - needle

licorice - sticks, black

licorice - sticks, red

string - or fishing line

toothpicks

alcohol, rubbing

blender

household item - enzyme-see teacher guide

household item - liquid detergent

household item - plastic container

peas - split- 100mL

salt - 1 mL

strainer

test tube

graduated cylinder

measuring cup

toothpicks - or other thin wood stick

water

household item - rubbing alcohol

household item - small glass (6-8 oz)

salt

soap - liquid

Keywords and Pronunciation

adenine (A-dn-een)

chromosomes (KROH-muh-sohms) : Thread-like structures made of protein and DNA which contain the instructions for building, maintaining, and operating the cell. Chromosomes contain the information that determines the eye, hair, skin color, and more in an individual.

cytosine (SIY-tuh-seen)

deoxyribonucleic (dee-AHK-sih-riy-boh-nyoo-clay-ick)

DNA : Deoxyribonucleic acid. This is the molecule, unique to each individual, carrying the genetic information to be found in every cell. All the information an organism needs to live and reproduce is contained in its DNA.

guanine (GWAH-neen)

thymine (THIY-meen)

LEARN

Activity 1. Optional: DNA--Instruction Manual for Life *(Online)*

It's almost too simple to be true. All of the instructions your cells need to carry out their functions are contained in one type of long molecule, called DNA. You'd think that DNA would have to be pretty complicated in order to do the job, but it's actually not. Learn about the twisted "double-helix" and four bases that make up DNA. Make a DNA model and then observe real DNA from a living thing.

Activity 2. Optional: Treat Yourself to DNA *(Offline)*

If someone told you they thought DNA was "twisted," you'd know the laugh was on them. DNA *is* twisted! Review the purpose and structure of DNA, and then build a candy model.

Safety

This lesson involves eating or working with food. Before beginning, check with your doctor, if necessary, to find out whether your student will have any allergic reaction to the food.
The needle (used in Activity 2) is sharp. Supervise your student if necessary.

Activity 3. Optional: Look at Real DNA *(Online)*

In three simple steps you can see real DNA from any living thing. Use detergent, enzymes, and alcohol to take out, or *extract*, DNA from split peas.

Safety

Wear safety goggles during Activity 3.
Activity 3 should be done with close supervision from an adult.

Activity 4. Optional: D-N-A from Y-O-U *(Offline)*

Since every cell in your body contains DNA, it is easy to extract and view your own DNA. You can do this by swishing water in your mouth to collect cells.

Materials

small glass, 180–240 mL (6-8 oz)
6% salt solution (mix 15 mL salt with 240 mL (8 oz) water)
10% solution of liquid soap (1 part soap to 9 parts water)
rubbing alcohol
toothpick

Procedure

1. Pour 15 mL salt-water solution into the juice glass and swirl it around your mouth for 30 seconds. The more vigorously you swirl, the more cheek cells you will collect.

2. Spit the water back into the glass.

3. Add 15 mL soap solution.

4. Mix by swirling very gently three or four times.

5. Gently add 15 mL rubbing alcohol. Try to pour it along the side of the glass so it forms a layer on top of the salt/water/soap solution.

6. Wait one minute.

7. Hold the glass up to the light and look for a cloudy, stringy substance forming at the bottom of the alcohol layer. You may see white bubbles. As the bubbles rise to the surface, you will begin to see white "strings" being drawn up along the bubbles. These strings are clumps containing thousands of DNA molecules.

8. Put the toothpick all the way down to the bottom of the glass and gently turn it in one direction. DO NOT STIR. The DNA will wrap around the rod and you can then put it in a smaller container.

What happened?

Adding soap to your cells breaks up a fatty membrane so the contents of the cells spill out. The salt makes it easy for the DNA to separate. DNA will not dissolve in alcohol, so when you add it to the solution, DNA collects where the two layers meet.

Name _____   Date _____

Treat Yourself to DNA

Scientists recognize that a long, thin, twisted molecule called *DNA* contains all the instructions for cells. Chromosomes are made up of DNA, like your body is made up of cells. These instructions include information about traits. If you've got brown eyes or are left-handed, you've got the instructions in your DNA to thank for that. Everyone all over the world is different from everyone else based on what is said in their DNA.

Learning about DNA takes a lot of hard work. A big break came in 1952 when a scientist named Rosalind Franklin produced pictures of DNA.

What does DNA look like? As you can see in the illustration, DNA has two strands that form a "double helix," a spiraling shape like a twisted ladder. DNA also has four bases: adenine, thymine, cytosine, and guanine.

When scientists model DNA, they generally use the same colors. Color the DNA illustration using the key.

Long chain links: red
Short chain links: black
Adenine: blue or aqua
Cytosine: red or crimson
Guanine: green
Thymine: tan

Treat Yourself to DNA

Notice that adenine and thymine are always paired together, as are guanine and cytosine. Notice, too, that the double helix in DNA is twisted.

Make a model

Use the illustration as a guide to make a DNA model.

Materials

licorice sticks, black
licorice sticks, red
fishing line or string, 2 pieces, 35 cm long
gumdrops, jelly beans, or marshmallows in colors close to red,
blue, green and tan (or white)
toothpicks
scissors
ruler (metric)
needle

Procedure

The Helix

1. Cut the black licorice into 18 small pieces, each about 1 cm long.
2. Cut the red licorice into 16 longer pieces, each 2 cm long.
3. Thread the needle with string or fishing line.
4. Start with the black licorice. Sew the string through the side of the black licorice.
5. Sew the string through the ends of the red licorice, so the red and black licorices are perpendicular.
6. On each line, string nine pieces of black licorice alternating with eight pieces of red. Wrap the string around the final piece of licorice so it does not fall off. You should have a total of 17 alternating pieces of licorice.
7. Lay the two lines side by side.

Treat Yourself to DNA

The Bases
1. Study the code for the bases:
   Adenine: blue or aqua candy
   Cytosine: red or crimson candy
   Guanine: green candy
   Thymine: tan or white candy
2. Make pairs of bases, connecting the candy with a toothpick. Slide the candy all the way to the middle of the toothpick.

The Molecule
3. Connect the bases to the red licorice pieces to make a ladder.
4. You do not have to attach the bases in any order, but make sure they are attached to the red licorice and that green always pairs with red and blue with tan.
5. Once you've attached your bases, gently lift the model in the air using two hands.
6. Twist your model slightly to see the double-helix structure of DNA.

Questions
1. How do the bases pair up in a DNA molecule? How does your model help you understand this? _____

_____

_____

_____

2. What makes one DNA molecule different from another? How could you change your DNA model to show changes among DNA molecules? _____

_____

_____

_____

3. Can DNA make an exact copy of itself? _____

4. How are chromosomes and DNA related? _____

Student Guide
Lesson 7. Optional: Heredity

This lesson is OPTIONAL. It's provided for enrichment or extra practice, but not required for completion of this unit. You may skip this lesson.

Lesson Objectives

- Explain that traits are passed from parents to offspring and are determined by genes, with an individual having two copies of each gene, one from each parent.
- Distinguish between dominant and recessive forms of genes.
- Use a Punnett square to determine the genetic combinations and traits possible in offspring of a simple genetic cross.

PREPARE

Approximate lesson time is 60 minutes.

Materials

For the Student

    🖴 Dominant and Recessive Traits

    household item - paper cup

    marker

    coins (3)

    tape - masking

    🖴 Inheritance

Keywords and Pronunciation

chromosomes (KROH-muh-sohms) : Thread-like structures, made of protein and DNA, that contain the instructions for building, maintaining, and operating the cell. Inherited traits are determined by the structure of the DNA that makes up the chromosomes.

genes : The parts of a chromosome that determine one or more characteristics, or groups of characteristics, that living things inherit from their parents. Genes determine your hair color, eye color, and more.

genetics (juh-NEH-tihks) : The study of how characteristics are passed on from parents to their offspring. Based on genetics, my daughter might have brown eyes like mine.

meiosis (miy-OH-suhs)

traits : Characteristics that vary from one individual to another. Inherited traits are passed on from parents to their offspring.

LEARN
Activity 1. Optional: Mendel and Genetics *(Online)*

Why do you look the way you do? Living things pass on copies of genetic material to their offspring. This material determines the way they look and function. Explore the role of genes and how they result in the passing of dominant and recessive traits. Learn to analyze how the forms of genes in parents affect the traits of their offspring. Survey other people for observable inherited traits.

Activity 2. Optional: Traits and Using a Punnett Square *(Offline)*

Explore the frequency of inheritance of genes and traits. Toss two parent coins, then analyze the outcome of their offspring.

Activity 3. Optional: Inheritance *(Online)*

What traits are most common? What is the relationship between how often a trait is observed and whether or not it is dominant? Conduct a survey of observable inherited traits in humans. Print the Inheritance activity sheet, then click the arrow to continue.

Name _____   Date _____

Dominant and Recessive Traits

You can use coins to find out about how genes and traits are inherited by offspring. *Traits* are characteristics that vary from one individual to the next. Genes, parts of the DNA molecule, determine what traits are passed on from one generation to the next.

Materials
masking tape
coins, 3
marker
paper cup

Procedure:
1. Place small pieces of masking tape on both sides of the coins.
2. Write a capital B on both sides of one coin. The B represents brown eyes. This coin represents a person with two genes for brown eyes.
3. On the other two coins, write a capital B on one side and a lowercase b on the other. These coins represent an individual with one gene for brown eyes (B) and one gene for blue eyes (b). These individuals are called "hybrid" because they have a mix of two forms of the eye color gene.

Which trait is dominant in this activity: brown eyes or blue?_____

4. Now you will "combine" the genes. Place the chip representing a parent with two genes for brown eyes (BB) and one chip that represents a hybrid parent (Bb) into the cup.
5. Cover the cup and shake it. Spill the coins onto a table.
6. The letters that are facing up represent the genes one offspring of the two parents will have.
7. Observe which letters are facing up. Make a tally mark in the box on the chart labeled "Test 1" to record the genes the offspring has.
8. Repeat steps 4 – 7 a total of 20 times.
9. Add up the number of checks in each box. Record the total for each box.
10. Repeat steps 4 – 8 using two hybrid (Bb) coins. Record your offspring in the chart labeled "Test 2."

Dominant and Recessive Traits

Observations

Test 1: BB x Bb

Parents	Offspring		
	BB (brown)	Bb (brown)	bb (blue)
BB x Bb			
Total after 20 tries			

Test 2: Bb X Bb

Parents	Offspring		
	BB (brown)	Bb (brown)	bb (blue)
Bb x Bb			
Total after 20 tries			

Using a Punnett Square

A *Punnett Square* is a tool that can be used to show possible ways genes from parents can combine in their offspring. It tells about *probability*, the chance something will happen. The letters stand for genes from each parent and are placed in the square first. Study the Punnett Square below.

Hybrid parent

Pure parent	B	b
B		
B		

B = brown-eyed gene
b = blue-eyed gene

Dominant and Recessive Traits

The next step is to combine the genes to show the possible ways they could be passed on to the offspring. Study the square to see this step. Circle the pairs of eye color genes that result in brown eyes. Put a triangle around the pairs that will result in blue eyes (none).

By looking at the square, you can see that each time the parents have offspring, there is a 100% chance that the offspring will have brown eyes.

Hybrid parent

Pure parent	B	b
B	BB	Bb
B	BB	Bb

B = brown-eyed gene
b = blue-eyed gene

Fill in the Punnett Square to the right to show the possible combinations of genes from two hybrid parents. Again, circle brown-eye pairs and put triangles around blue-eyed pairs.

Hybrid parent

Hybrid parent	B	b
B		
b		

B = brown-eyed gene
b = blue-eyed gene

When these parents have offspring, what is the probability that the offspring will have brown eyes? _____
When these parents have offspring, what is the probability that the offspring will have blue eyes? _____

Analysis

Look back at your observations from your tests.

1. In 20 test pairings, how many test offspring from a pure brown-eyed parent (BB) and a hybrid brown-eyed parent (Bb) had brown eyes? _____ How many had blue? _____

2. In 20 test pairings, how many test offspring from two hybrid brown-eyed parents (Bb and Bb) had brown eyes? _____ How many had blue? _____

Dominant and Recessive Traits

3. Look back at your Punnett Squares. In Test 1, did you find that 100% of the offspring had brown eyes? _____

4. The Punnett Square for Test 2 says there is a 75% chance the offspring will have brown eyes and a 25% chance the offspring will have blue eyes. If you performed Test 2 a total of 100 times, would you expect exactly 75 offspring to have brown eyes and exactly 25 offspring to have blue? Why or why not?_____

_____

_____

_____

_____

5. How would your results be different if you tossed a hybrid coin (Bb) and a recessive coin (bb)? Make and complete a Punnett Square to answer the question._____

_____

_____

_____

6. If you have time, try it.

Name _____   Date _____

Inheritance

Eye color is just one of many interesting inherited traits. Survey a group of people to find out which traits are more common than others.

Hypothesis

Study the photos of inherited traits. You will survey 10 people about their traits. Which of the traits do you think will be the most common? Write a hypothesis._____

_____

Materials

paper
pencil
Example of Inherited Traits sheet

Procedure:

1. Study the examples of inherited traits.
2. Survey 10 people. Try to survey people other than family members.
3. Observe which form of each trait each person has.
4. Record your data in the chart. Make a tally mark for each person by the appropriate trait he or she has.

Observations

Trait	Tally
Dimples	
No dimples	
Hitchhiker's Thumb	
Regular thumb	
Can curl tongue	
Cannot curl tongue	
Short second toe	
Long second toe	
Left thumb on top when folding hands	
Right thumb on top when folding hands	
Unattached earlobe	
Attached earlobe	
Can make a "V" with fingers	
Cannot make a "V" with fingers	

Inheritance

Analysis

Use the data from your observations to make a bar graph of a few traits.

10					
9					
8					
7					
6					
5					
4					
3					
2					
1					
dimples	no dimples	can curl tongue	cannot curl tongue	unattached earlobe	attached earlobe

Conclusion

1. Which traits were most common?_____

_____

2. Because a trait is most common, does that mean it is dominant? For example, the gene for six fingers is dominant. You probably do not know many six-fingered people. Study the table below to help you answer the question. _____

_____

_____

_____

Inheritance

Study the list of traits below.

	Dominant	Recessive
Earlobes	Unattached (F) (free)	Attached (f)
Dimples	Dimples (D)	No dimples (d)
Thumb	Hitchhiker's Thumb (H)	Regular thumb (h)
Tongue-rolling	Roller (R)	Nonroller (r)

3. Choose one of the traits for which to make a Punnett Square. You may cross pure parents or hybrid parents. Explain the results of your Punnett Square. _____

_____

_____

Student Guide
Lesson 8: Unit Review and Assessment

Play Cell-ebrity Pranksters to review cell structures and processes. Review organelles, the movement of molecules, photosynthesis, and respiration. Then take the unit assessment.

Lesson Objectives

- Demonstrate knowledge and skills gained in this unit.
- Describe the three major ideas of the cell theory.
- Distinguish between plant and animal cells.
- Identify the major structures of cells and describe their functions (nucleus, cytoplasm, cell wall, cell membrane, chromosomes, mitochondria, and chloroplasts).
- Explain that different types of substances move across the cell membrane by means of diffusion, osmosis, and active transport.
- Explain that plant cells store energy through photosynthesis and that plant and animal cells release stored energy during respiration.
- Identify the major structures of the cell (such as cell membrane, cytoplasm, and nucleus) and describe their functions.
- Recognize various ways in which molecules are transported across the cell membrane.
- Describe the process of *photosynthesis* in plants.
- Recognize the major cell organelles (for example, endoplasmic reticulum, ribosomes, Golgi bodies, chloroplasts, chromosomes, mitochondria, and vacuoles) and describe their functions.
- Define *diffusion* as the process by which molecules move from areas of higher concentration to areas of lower concentration.
- Recognize that water moves through membranes by *osmosis*--diffusion of water through a semipermeable membrane.
- Explain that all the information an organism needs to live and reproduce is contained in its DNA.
- Demonstrate mastery of the skill taught in this unit.

PREPARE

Approximate lesson time is 60 minutes.

Materials

　　For the Student

　　　　🖳 Question Review Table

LEARN
Activity 1: Cell-ebrity Pranksters *(Online)*

ASSESS
Unit Assessment: Cells and Cell Processes (*Online*)
Complete an offline Unit Assessment. Your learning coach will score this part of the Assessment.

LEARN
Activity 2. Optional: Unit Assessment Review Table *(Online)*
If you earned a score of **less than 80%** on the Unit Assessment, complete the activity.

If you earned a score of **80% or greater**, you may skip this activity.

Let's prepare to retake the Unit Assessment:
- Print the Question Review Table.
- Identify the questions that you answered incorrectly.
- Complete the appropriate review activities listed in the table.

Note: This will guide you through the process of using the Unit Assessment Review Tables. You may skip this video if you've already viewed it in another unit or course. As always, check in with your student's teacher if you have any questions.

Activity 3. Optional: ZlugQuest Measurement *(Online)*

Name _____   Date _____

Unit Assessment

Select the answer that best completes the question. (1 point each)

1. Movement of molecules from an area of higher concentration to one of lower concentration is called _____.
   A. osmosis
   B. mitosis
   C. diffusion
   D. active transport

2. Movement of molecules from an area of lower concentration to one of higher concentration with carrier molecules, using energy, is called _____.
   A. osmosis
   B. mitosis
   C. diffusion
   D. active transport

3. Diffusion of water across a membrane is called _____.
   A. osmosis
   B. mitosis
   C. cytokinesis
   D. active transport

4. DNA is found in the _____.
   A. vacuole
   B. chromosomes
   C. cell membrane
   D. Golgi body

Unit Assessment

Word Bank

cells	traits	living	photosynthesis
respiration	DNA	cell	non-living

Use words from the word bank to complete the sentences. (2 points each)

5. All living things are made of _____.

6. Inside the chromosomes are molecules that contain all information an organism needs to grow and reproduce. This is its _____.

7. The _____ is the basic unit of structure and function in living things.

8. Plant cells change the sun's energy to chemical energy during _____.

9. Living cells come only from other _____ cells.

10. Cells change chemical energy into something usable during _____.

11. Study the cell diagram and the chart. Label the organelles based on their descriptions. Fill in any missing descriptions in the chart. (1 point each)
    A-nucleus
    B-chloroplast
    C-mitochondria
    D-vacuole
    E-cell membrane
    F-cell wall

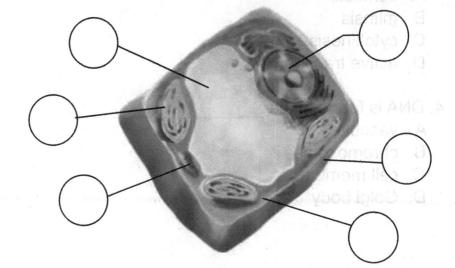

Unit Assessment

12. Fill in the description or the name of the organelle. (2 points each)

	Cell Organelle	Description
A	Nucleus	
B		in plants, changes sunlight energy into chemical energy through photosynthesis
C		changes chemical energy into energy that is useable by the cell
D		fluid filled bubbles that store and digest food, get rid of waste, and pump water
E		contains the genetic information for the cell and DNA
F	cell membrane	
G		rigid, gives plant cells their shape and support

Unit Assessment

13. Read the following notes a student took about cells. Cross out any incorrect items and re-write them in the correct spot. Do not add any items. (1 point for each correctly changed item)

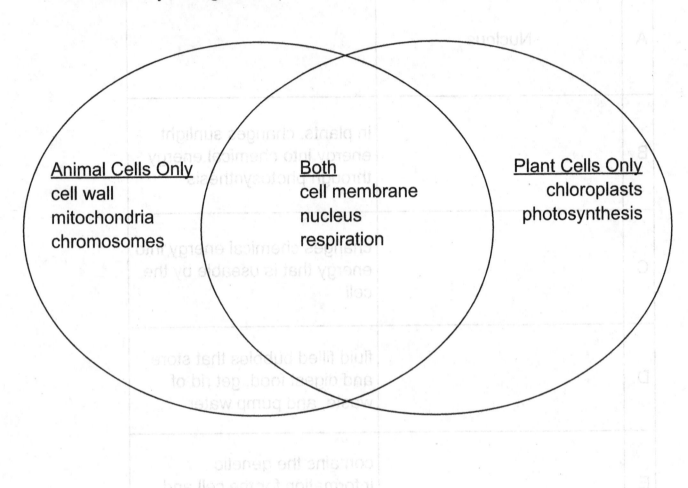

Animal Cells Only
cell wall
mitochondria
chromosomes

Both
cell membrane
nucleus
respiration

Plant Cells Only
chloroplasts
photosynthesis

Assessment Date _____

Unit 6: Cells and Cell Processes

Before you retake the Unit Assessment, use the table to figure out which activities you should review.

Question Review Table

Circle the numbers of the questions that you missed on the Unit Assessment. Review the activities that correspond with these questions.

Question	Lesson	Review Activity
1	3: Diffusion, Osmosis, and Active Transport	Explore: Moving Through Membranes Osmosis
2	3: Diffusion, Osmosis, and Active Transport	Explore: Moving Through Membranes
3	3: Diffusion, Osmosis, and Active Transport	Explore: Moving Through Membranes Diffusion Through a Membrane
5,7,9	1: The Cell Theory	Explore: What Are You Made Of? Cell Record Observe Human Cells
6	6: DNA	Explore: DNA-Instruction Manual for Life Look at Real DNA D-N-A from Y-O-U
8	4: Photosynthesis and Respiration	Explore: Energy Flows Photosynthesis and Respiration Review Gas Exchange in Plants
10	4: Photosynthesis and Respiration	Explore: Energy Flows Photosynthesis and Respiration Review Exhale!
4,11,12,13,14	2: Cell Organelles	Explore: Inside a Cell This is Your Life, Cell! A Cell You Can Eat Visit a Virtual Cell

Assessment _____ Date _____

Unit 6: Cells and Cell Processes

Before you retake the Unit Assessment, use the table to figure out which activities you should review.

Question Review Table

Circle the numbers of the questions that you missed on the Unit Assessment. Review the activities that correspond with these questions.

Question	Lesson	Review Activity
1	3. Diffusion, Osmosis, and Active Transport	Explore: Moving Through Membranes; Osmosis
2	3. Diffusion, Osmosis, and Active Transport	Explore: Moving Through Membranes
3	3. Diffusion, Osmosis, and Active Transport	Explore: Moving Through Membranes; Diffusion Through a Membrane
5, 7, 9	1. The Cell Theory	Explore: What Are You Made Of?; Cell Record; Observe Human Cells
6	6. DNA	Explore: DNA Instruction Manual for Life; Look at Real DNA; U-(14) from Y-O-U
8	4. Photosynthesis and Respiration	Explore: Energy Flows Photosynthesis and Respiration Review; Gas Exchange in Plants
10	4. Photosynthesis and Respiration	Explore: Energy Flows Photosynthesis and Respiration Review; Exhale!
4, 11, 12, 13, 14	2. Cell Organelles	Explore: Inside a Cell; This is Your Life, Cell!; A Cell You Can Eat; Visit a Virtual Cell

Student Guide
Lesson 1: Naming and Classifying Life

Lesson Objectives

- State that Carolus Linnaeus developed a system for naming and classifying organisms that is still used today.
- Recognize that an organism's scientific name is made up of the genus and species the organism belongs to.

PREPARE

Approximate lesson time is 60 minutes.

Advance Preparation

- If you have not yet received the book *The Kingdoms of Life: Classification*, skip to the next unit. Return to this one when the book arrives.

Materials

For the Student

Come Learn with Me: The Kingdoms of Life: Classification by Bridget Anderson

📖 Scientific Classification Crossword Puzzle

Keywords and Pronunciation

Aristotle (AIR-uh-stah-tl)

Carolus Linnaeus (kah-raw-LOUS lih-NEE-uhs)

genus (JEE-nuhs)

species (SPEE-sheez)

LEARN
Activity 1: Let's Read *(Online)*

There are many forms of life in the world. Some are so tiny that you can't see them without a microscope. How do we make sense of all these different organisms? To study them, scientists classify them by their characteristics. Learn how scientists do this. Read pages 6 through 11 of *The Kingdoms of Life: Classification*.

Activity 2: Scientific Classification Crossword *(Offline)*

Do you have a good understanding of scientific classification? Prove this to yourself by solving the Scientific Classification Crossword Puzzle.

ASSESS

Lesson Assessment: Naming and Classifying Life (*Online*)

You will complete an online assessment covering the main objectives of this lesson. Your assessment will be scored by the computer.

Name _____ Date _____

Scientific Classification Crossword Puzzle

Use the clues on the next page to complete the puzzle.

Scientific Classification Crossword Puzzle

ACROSS

2. This genus means *catlike animals*.
5. He was an ancient Greek philosopher who divided plants and animals into categories.
10. This Latin word means *appearance* or *kind*. It is the second part of the scientific name for an organism.
11. Linnaeus named species either in Latin or in this language.
13. This scientific term for *baby* can be applied both to plants and to animals.
14. First name of Linnaeus, a scientist who is famous for his system of classification.

DOWN

1. The process of grouping things according to the characteristics they share.
3. This Swedish biologist developed a system for classifying organisms.
4. Group of related species. The first part of a scientific name for an organism refers to this.
6. So far, scienifists have identified more than ___ million kinds of organisms.
7. A place where books are classified.
8. Aristotle classified plants as herbs, shrubs, or ___.
9. Farmers classify farm animals and plants according to this.
12. Its scientific name is *Canis familiarus*.

Student Guide
Lesson 2: The Tools of Taxonomy

How does a classification system work? Learn more about Carolus Linnaeus, who led the way to the current system of classification that groups organisms according to their shared characteristics.

Lesson Objectives

- Recognize that living things are classified by shared characteristics.
- Identify the seven major levels of classification: Kingdom, Phylum, Class, Order, Family, Genus, and Species.

PREPARE

Approximate lesson time is 60 minutes.

Materials

  For the Student

  Come Learn with Me: The Kingdoms of Life: Classification by Bridget Anderson

  💻 Trees of the Pacific Northwest

Keywords and Pronunciation

Anton van Leeuwenhoek (AHN-tohn vahn LAY-ven-hook)

Carolus Linnaeus (kah-raw-LOUS lih-NEE-uhs)

conifer (KAH-nuh-fur)

dichotomous (diy-KAH-tuh-muhs)

genus (JEE-nuhs)

phylum (FIY-luhm)

species (SPEE-sheez)

LEARN
Activity 1: Let's Read *(Online)*

Activity 2: Identifying Trees *(Online)*
Try your hand at identifying trees of the Pacific Northwest using a dichotomous key.

ASSESS

Lesson Assessment: The Tools of Taxonomy (*Online*)
You will complete an online assessment covering the main goals of this lesson. Your assessment will be scored by the computer.

LEARN
Activity 3. Optional: Dichotomous Keys *(Online)*

This Activity is OPTIONAL. It's provided for enrichment or extra practice, but not required for completion of this lesson. You may skip this activity.

Learn about Dichotomous Keying.

Name _____   Date _____

Trees of the Pacific Northwest

Try your hand at identifying trees of the Pacific Northwest using a dichotomous key.

The needle-like leaves are not clustered on this tree. The needles are longer than 1/2 inch. The tiny pegs on the twigs are squared with sharp needles. _____

This tree has leaves that are needle-like. The needles are clustered with 2-5 needles. _____

The needle-like leaves on this tree are not clustered and are longer than 1/2 inch. There are no pegs on the twigs. The buds are small and pointed, and they are not found clustered on the twig. As you turn the pointed needle over, it is white underneath. _____

The flattened leaves on this tree are scale-like. All of the leaves are short and sharp. _____

The needle-like leaves, which measure longer than 1/2 inch, are not clustered. There are no pegs on the twigs. The buds are not large but are pointed. The terminal buds are not clustered. As you turn the needle over, it is green underneath. _____

Student Guide
Lesson 3: Phylogenetic Trees and the Kingdoms of Life

Scientists classify all life on Earth into one of six kingdoms. Join the classification adventure and find out what the six kingdoms are!

Lesson Objectives

- Name the six kingdoms: Archaebacteria, Eubacteria, Protista, Fungi, Planta, and Animalia.

PREPARE

Approximate lesson time is 60 minutes.

Materials

> For the Student
>
> > Come Learn with Me: The Kingdoms of Life: Classification by Bridget Anderson
> >
> > 📖 What Would Linnaeus Say?

Keywords and Pronunciation

Animalia (A-nuh-MAY-lee-uh)

archaebacteria (AHR-kee-bak-TIHR-ee-uh)

eubacteria (YOO-bak-TIHR-ee-uh)

fungi (FUN-jiy)

genetics (juh-NEH-tihks) : The study of how characteristics are passed on from parents to their offspring. Based on genetics, my daughter might have brown eyes like mine.

phylogenetic (fiy-loh-juh-NEH-tihk)

Protista (proh-TIS-tuh)

LEARN
Activity 1: Let's Read (Online)

The science of *genetics* explains why some organisms are more similar than others. It also explains why members of the same families tend to have similar characteristics--they may look alike, act alike, or both. Read pages 16 through 19 of *The Kingdoms of Life: Classification*.

Activity 2: What Would Linnaeus Say? (Offline)

Genetic relationships explain a lot about how like or unlike organisms can be. Which organisms are closely related and which are distant? What kinds of living creatures belong to each of the kingdoms? With the help of your book, *you* can give the same answers Linnaeus would give.

ASSESS

Lesson Assessment: Phylogenetic Trees and the Kingdoms of Life (*Online*)

You will complete an online assessment covering the main goals of this lesson. Your assessment will be scored by the computer.

Name _____   Date _____

What Would Linnaeus Say?

A. For each organism listed below, circle the organism that is more closely related genetically. (Hint: use the diagram in your book for help.)

1. **human girl**	human man	female duck
2. **sunflower**	worm	daisy
3. **green algae**	moss	cnidarian
4. **snake**	lizard	flatworm
5. **crustacean**	insect	fungi

B. Use the Word Bank below to complete this paragraph.

Word Bank

genetics   fossils   phylogenetic tree   different   similar   identical

The branch of science that studies relationships between

organisms is _____. Children in the same family have

nearly _____ genes, while birds and insects have very

_____ genes. Once genetic relationships are understood,

scientists can show the relationships by drawing a _____

_____. By studying genes from _____ and genes

from animals living today, scientists gain evidence about how

modern organisms are related to ancient organisms.

What Would Linnaeus Say?

C. Matching: Draw lines to connect the name of each kingdom with its description.

Kingdom
Archaebacteria

They live in wet places. Examples are algae and slime molds.

Kingdom
Eubacteria

Their cells use chlorophyll to help them make their own food.

Kingdom
Protista

These single-cell organisms live in extreme environments, such as deep-sea vents.

Kingdom Fungi

Fish, insects, and mammals belong to this kingdom.

Kingdom Planta

These common bacteria are found everywhere on Earth.

Kingdom Animalia

These eukaryotic organisms absorb nutrients from dead or living plants and animals.

Student Guide
Lesson 4: Kingdom Archaebacteria

Do you know of any organisms that live in the most extreme environments on Earth? Scientists have found bacteria from Kingdom Archaebacteria in the coldest and hottest places on Earth. Get out your microscope and take a closer look at these fascinating organisms.

Lesson Objectives

- Identify two characteristics common to organisms in Kingdom Archaebacteria (live without oxygen, live in extreme environments both hot and cold).
- Identify one organism in Kingdom Archaebacteria.

PREPARE

Approximate lesson time is 60 minutes.

Materials

For the Student

Come Learn with Me: The Kingdoms of Life: Classification by Bridget Anderson

📖 Solving the Riddles of Bacteria

Keywords and Pronunciation

archaebacteria (AHR-kee-bak-TIHR-ee-uh)

cyanobacteria (siy-A-nuh-bak-TIHR-ee-uh)

eubacteria (YOO-bak-TIHR-ee-uh)

halophile (HA-luh-fiyl)

methanogen (muh-THAN-uh-juhn)

LEARN

Activity 1: Let's Read *(Online)*

Archaebacteria may be tiny, but they can adapt extremely well to different environments. Learn how these tiny creatures survive in some of the harshest places in the world. Read pages 20 through 21 of *The Kingdoms of Life: Classification*.

Activity 2: Bacteria Riddles *(Offline)*

Are you good at riddles? With the help of your book, you'll be able to solve the riddles of these bacteria.

ASSESS

Lesson Assessment: Kingdom Archaebacteria (*Online*)

You will complete an online assessment covering the main goals of this lesson. Your assessment will be scored by the computer.

Name _____   Date _____

Solving the Riddles of Bacteria

Read each riddle, then solve it. (Hint: You'll find help in your text.)

1. I am shaped like a rod, and I live in the intestines of animals. What kind of bacteria am I? (Hint: my name starts with the letter S.)

   _____

2. If you've ever had a "strep throat," then I was responsible. I am the bacteria that causes throat infections. Who am I?

   _____

3. I love hot environments--even the hottest ones! I can also live without oxygen. What kind of bacteria am I?

   _____

4. All bacteria are made up of me. I am a type of cell. Who am I?

   _____

5. Because I can live in extremely salty environments, I can live in the Great Salt Lake in Utah. What kind of bacteria am I?

   _____

6. If you want to see the structure and behavior of bacteria, you need to use me. (I'm not just an ordinary microscope!)

   _____

7. I am a disease caused by the dangerous bacteria called *Borrelia burgdofferri*. _____.

SUPER CHALLENGE: Name this term! The first one has been done for you.

1. All rod-shaped bacteria are called **bacillus** _____.
2. All round bacteria are called _____.
3. All spiral bacteria are called _____.
4. This term refers to things that love extreme environments. Archaeophiles are one example. _____.

Student Guide
Lesson 5: Kingdom Eubacteria

All bacteria that are not part of Kingdom Archaebacteria are members of Kingdom Eubacteria. Look deep into the microscopic world and discover the eubacteria that live near us, even within our own bodies!

Lesson Objectives

- Identify a characteristic common to organisms in Kingdom Eubacteria (live in less extreme environments).
- Identify one organism in Kingdom Eubacteria.

PREPARE

Approximate lesson time is 60 minutes.

Materials

For the Student

Come Learn with Me: The Kingdoms of Life: Classification by Bridget Anderson

Name That Eubacteria or Virus!

Keywords and Pronunciation

amoeba (uh-MEE-buh)

cyanobacteria (siy-A-nuh-bak-TIHR-ee-uh)

eubacteria (YOO-bak-TIHR-ee-uh)

paramecium (PAIR-uh-MEE-shee-uhm)

thermophile (THUR-muh-fiyl)

LEARN
Activity 1: Let's Read *(Online)*

Eubacteria may be invisible to the naked eye, but they play a very important role in our lives. Some are very helpful, while others are quite dangerous. Read pages 22 through 23 of *The Kingdoms of Life: Classification*.

Activity 2: Name That Eubacteria or Virus! *(Offline)*

Members of Kingdom Eubacteria are known as the *true bacteria*. These organisms obtain nutrients in very different--sometimes unusual--ways. Read the clues, and then name the kind of eubacteria they describe.

ASSESS

Lesson Assessment: Kingdom Eubacteria (*Online*)

You will complete an online assessment covering the main objectives of this lesson. Your assessment will be scored by the computer.

LEARN

Activity 3. Optional: Microbiologists Do! (*Online*)

This activity is OPTIONAL. It's provided for enrichment or extra practice, but not required for completion of this lesson. You may skip this activity.

Have you ever wondered what kind of scientists study bacteria and other microscopic organisms? Microbiologists do. Discover the exciting lives they lead, and solve Microbe Mysteries online.

Name _____ Date _____

Name That Eubacteria or Virus!

Read each description, then write *photo-autotroph*, *chemo-autotroph*, *heterotroph*, or *virus* in the space next to each.

1. Decomposers are members of this group. _____

2. Some of these are considered "nitrogen-fixing machines." _____

3. Not all scientists think these are even alive. _____

4. They make their food from sunlight. _____

5. To reproduce, they must use the cell of another organism. _____

6. Sulfur, iron, and nitrogen are needed to make food for this group. _____

7. They contain chlorophyll. _____

8. They absorb nutrients from other organisms because they can't make their own food. _____

9. Their bodies are not made of cells, though they can use the cells of others. _____

10. Photosynthesis lets them make food. _____

11. Parasites are part of this group. _____

12. These are not actually bacteria. _____

13. Their name means "self-nourishment from chemicals." _____

14. Cyanobacteria are part of this group. _____

Student Guide
Lesson 6: Kingdom Protista

Many members of Kingdom Protista are one-celled organisms that live in wet environments. Amoebas, paramecia, molds, and algae are all part of this group. Find out about some of the types of protists and learn about these organisms that are all around you.

Lesson Objectives

- Identify two characteristics common to organisms in Kingdom Protista (thrive in wet environments, most are single celled).
- Identify two organisms in Kingdom Protista (protozoa, amoeba, paramecium, algae, seaweed, water mold, slime mold).
- State that protists are often grouped according to whether they are plant-like, fungus-like or animal-like.

PREPARE

Approximate lesson time is 60 minutes.

Advance Preparation

- You will need 10 jars and 20 cups of distilled water for the optional Soap and Algae activity.

Materials

For the Student

Come Learn with Me: The Kingdoms of Life: Classification by Bridget Anderson

🖳 Protists by Alphabet

Optional

🖳 How Does Soap Affect Algae Growth?

jar, storage (10)

measuring cup

soap - 1 1/2 cups of liquid soap

spoon - measuring

water - distilled, 20 cups

water - lake, stream, tap, or bay, 20 cups

water - tap

Keywords and Pronunciation

algae (AL-jee)
amoeba (uh-MEE-buh)
eukaryotic (yoo-KAHR-ee-AH-tihk)
fungi (FUN-jiy)
paramecium (PAIR-uh-MEE-shee-uhm)
Protista (proh-TIS-tuh)
protozoa (proh-tuh-ZOH-uh)

LEARN
Activity 1: Let's Read *(Online)*

Many members of Kingdom Protista are made of only one cell, while others are multicellular. Discover *protists*--the eukaryotic organisms that live in oceans, land, and lakes, as well as inside other organisms. Read pages 24 through 27 of *The Kingdoms of Life: Classification*.

Activity 2: Protists by Alphabet *(Offline)*

There are many protists. Use alphabet clues to solve the Protists by Alphabet puzzle.

ASSESS
Lesson Assessment: Kingdom Protista (*Online*)

You will complete an online assessment covering the main goals of this lesson. Your assessment will be scored by the computer.

LEARN
Activity 3. Optional: Soap and Algae *(Offline)*

This activity is OPTIONAL. It's provided for enrichment or extra practice, but not required for completion of this lesson. You may skip this activity.

You already know that algae grow in water. What do you think would happen if you added soap to the water? Find out!

Name _____   Date _____

Protists by Alphabet

Read the clues, then fill in the answer. The first letter of each answer is given for you. Some of the answers have been completed for you.

A_____ look like jelly. To move, they have to change shape.

B_____ and pieces of dead organisms are food for slime molds.

C_____ are covered with little hairs. They move in a corkscrew fashion.

D_____ _____ have killed a lot of crops. The rotten potato in your book is infected with it.

E_____ _____ grows on a stick. There is a picture of one in your book.

F_____ move by flapping flagella. Many are parasitic.

G_____ can look furry when water molds grow on them. There is a picture of one in your book.

H_____ is one way to describe a paramecium. Its many cilia make it look this way.

I_____ _____ _____ is a famous disaster that took place in the 1840s. A downy mildew caused it to happen.

Jelly-like_____ blobs are one way the book describes amoebas.

K_____ is a large, complex type of algae that can grow into forests underwater.

Protists by Alphabet

L_____ and oceans are home to the Kingdom Protista.

M_____ described in your book are slime and water.

N_____ is the Japanese name for a kind of seaweed called Porphyra nereocystis.

O_____ is produced by algae. Humans need it to breathe.

P_____ is a very complex protozoan.

Q is not the first letter of any protist in your book.

R_____, brown, and green are some of the colors algae can have.

S_____ live in the cells of other living things. They are very tiny parasites.

T_____ is how the bodies of amoebas and most protists look, which means you can see through them.

U_____ is also called sea lettuce. It is a kind of alga.

Vorticella_____ is a ciliate. It is not mentioned in your book.

W_____ _____ look like cotton. Some grow on dead algae, and some grow on living organisms.

X is not the first letter of any of the words in this section.

Yamadaella caenomyce is a kind of algae that grows in the Red Sea, but it is not shown in your book.

Zoomastiginia is the group that flagellates belong to. (This information is not in the book.)

Name _____   Date _____

How Does Soap Affect Algae Growth?

How do you think soap would affect the growth of algae? Could you guess? The experiment will answer the question.

1. Fill five jars with 950mL each of distilled water. Label the jars 1, 2, 3, 4, and 5.

2. In a bowl, mix 240mL of water with 360mLof liquid soap.

3. Pour 30mL of soapy water from the bowl in jar #2, 60mL in jar #3, 90mL in jar #4, and 120mL in jar #5.

4. Fill five different jars with 950mL of lake, stream, tap or bay water. Then label the jars 6, 7, 8, 9, and 10.

5. Pour 30mL of soapy water in jar #7, 60mL in jar #8, 90mL in jar #9, and 120mL in jar #10.

6. Place all of the jars in a location with plenty of sunlight.

For the next five days, record your observations of odor and color change in the observation sheet provided. After the five days, place a 10cm strip of unlined white paper behind each jar. Look through the liquid in the jar and identify the jar that has the most algae.

How Does Soap Affect Algae Growth?

OBSERVATION SHEET

Distilled Water					
	DAY 1	DAY 2	DAY 3	DAY 4	DAY 5
Jar 1: Color					
Odor					
Jar 2: Color					
Odor					
Jar 3: Color					
Odor					
Jar 4: Color					
Odor					
Jar 5: Color					
Odor					

Lake, Stream, Tap, or Bay Water					
	DAY 1	DAY 2	DAY 3	DAY 4	DAY 5
Jar 6: Color					
Odor					
Jar 7: Color					
Odor					
Jar 8: Color					
Odor					
Jar 9: Color					
Odor					
Jar 10: Color					
Odor					

Student Guide
Lesson 7: Kingdom Fungi

Have you ever seen a piece of fruit with fuzz on it? Do you like mushrooms on your pizza? The fuzz and the mushrooms are both fungi! Look deeper into the diverse world of Kingdom Fungi.

Lesson Objectives

- Identify characteristics common to organisms in Kingdom Fungi (grow best in warm, moist conditions; reproduce through spores).
- Identify two organisms in Kingdom Fungi (mushroom, lichens, some molds, yeast).

PREPARE

Approximate lesson time is 60 minutes.

Advance Preparation

- If you choose to do the Rising Yeast optional activity, plan to set aside about an hour and twenty minutes for it.

Materials

For the Student

    Come Learn with Me: The Kingdoms of Life: Classification by Bridget Anderson

    📖 Spreading Spores

    clay

    cotton ball (8)

    stick

    balloon - long and slender

    tape

Optional

    📖 Rising Yeast

    food - cup of flour (2)

    food - pkg. of rapid-rise yeast

    food - tsp. honey (6)

    food - tsp. sugar (6)

    household item - clothespins (24)

    household item - drinking straws (24)

    household item - medium-sized bowls (4)

    stopwatch - watch or timer

    measuring cup

    ruler, metric

    spoon

    spoon - measuring

Keywords and Pronunciation

fungi (FUN-jiy)
fungus (FUNG-guhs)

LEARN
Activity 1: Let's Read *(Online)*

Toadstools, mushrooms, and molds are all part of Kingdom Fungi. Learn about the many types of fungi. Read pages 28 through 29 of *The Kingdoms of Life: Classification*.

Activity 2: Spreading Spores *(Offline)*

Create your own model of a black bread mold, which is a type of fungus. Learn how its spores spread.

ASSESS
Lesson Assessment: Kingdom Fungi (*Online*)

You will complete an online assessment covering the main goals of this lesson. Your assessment will be scored by the computer.

LEARN
Activity 3. Optional: Rising Yeast *(Offline)*

This activity is OPTIONAL. It's provided for enrichment or extra practice, but not required for completion of this lesson. You may skip this activity.

Did you ever wonder why you have to add yeast to the flour when you make bread? Have you wondered how the other ingredients affect the way yeast works? Cook up your own experiment to find out!

Name _____   Date _____

Spreading Spores

Do you know how spores spread? To find out, create this model.

Materials

long, slender balloon   cotton balls
tape   stick
clay - any color   permanent marker

Procedure

1. Stretch the balloon so that it will inflate easily. Don't inflate it or tie off the end yet.

2. Make 8 balls from the cotton that are no more than 1 cm in diameter. Put them in the neck of the balloon.

3. Inflate the balloon and tie it off with a knot on the end.

4. Tape the tied end of the balloon to the stick.

5. Put the bottom of the stick into the clay. Shape the clay around the end of the stick so that it stands up.

   This is a model of the spore-bearing structure of a bread mold. The balloon is the spore case, and the cotton balls are the spores.

6. Carefully poke the balloon with the pin. This is similar to how the spores of a mold get spread.

Conclusions

If these were real spores, what would happen next? _____

_____

Name _____   Date _____

Rising Yeast

Do you know why people use yeast to make bread? Have you ever wondered what affects the behavior of yeast? Here's your chance to find out!

Materials

2 cups of flour (plus a little extra)	24 clothespins
4 medium-sized bowls	measuring spoons
1 package of rapid-rise yeast	¼ cup measuring cup
access to warm water	spoon
6 teaspoons of sugar	metric ruler
honey	permanent marking pen
24 clear drinking straws	clock, watch, or timer

Procedure

1. Using the ruler, measure the point 3 cm from one end of each straw. Use the permanent marker to mark that point with a line.

2. Put ¼ cup of flour into each of the two bowls. Mark the first bowl as the "Control" and the second bowl as 1.

3. Pour ¼ teaspoon of yeast into each of the bowl marked 1 (do not put yeast into the bowl labeled "Control"). Using the spoon, stir together the ingredients in each bowl. Start with the Control bowl.

4. Fill a cup with warm water from your faucet. The water should be warm, not hot and steaming. Dust your hands with a little flour. Carefully add the water to the control bowl about a teaspoonful at a time and begin to knead the mixture. Your dough should eventually feel damp, not wet. Form the dough into a ball.

5. Repeat step 4 with each the remaining bowl, working as quickly as you can.

Rising Yeast

6. Working quickly, push three straws in and out of the Control dough until the dough inside the straw reaches the 3-centimeter mark. Lay these straws by the Control bowl. Repeat this step with each of the remaining bowls. Be sure to keep the straws beside the right bowls and don't mix them up.

7. Now pinch the bottoms of each of your Control dough straws, pushing the dough up from the bottom enough to clip a clothespin to the end of each straw. Mark the new height of the dough on each straw. Stand the straws upright using the clothespins as bases. Do the same with the rest of the straws. Label the batches of straws as Control and 1.

8. Mark the time on your clock or watch or set your timer for 10 minutes. Wait 10 minutes. Then mark the heights of the dough in each straw. Repeat this step 10 minutes later. Repeat after another 10 minutes has passed.

9. Throw out the straws and dough, then wash the bowls.

10. Record your results.

12. Repeat the procedure but this time you will be adding sugar and additional bowls.

Procedure

1. Using the ruler, measure the point 3 cm from one end of each straw. Use the permanent marker to mark that point with a line.

2. Put ¼ cup of flour into each of the four bowls. Mark the first bowl as the "Control." Mark the others as 1, 2, and 3.

3. Measure 1 teaspoon of sugar and add it to the flour in bowl 1. Put 2 teaspoons of sugar into bowl 2. Put 3 teaspoons of sugar into bowl 3.

4. Pour ¼ teaspoon of yeast into each of the four bowls. Using the spoon, stir together the ingredients in each bowl. Start with the Control bowl.

Rising Yeast

5. Fill a cup with warm water from your faucet. The water should be warm, not hot and steaming. Dust your hands with a little flour. Carefully add the water to the control bowl about a teaspoonful at a time and begin to knead the mixture. Your dough should eventually feel damp, not wet. Form the dough into a ball.

6. Repeat step 5 with each of the remaining bowls, working as quickly as you can.

7. Working quickly, push three straws in and out of the Control dough until the dough inside the straw reaches the 3-centimeter mark. Lay these straws by the Control bowl. Repeat this step with each of the remaining bowls. Be sure to keep the straws beside the right bowls and don't mix them up.

8. Now pinch the bottoms of each of your Control dough straws, pushing the dough up from the bottom enough to clip a clothespin to the end of each straw. Mark the new height of the dough on each straw. Stand the straws upright using the clothespins as bases. Do the same with the rest of the straws. Label the batches of straws as Control, 1, 2, and 3.

9. Mark the time on your clock or watch or set your timer for 10 minutes. Wait 10 minutes. Then mark the heights of the dough in each straw. Repeat this step 10 minutes later. Repeat after another 10 minutes has passed.

10. Throw out the straws and dough; then wash the bowls.

11. Repeat the experiment one last time: this time, substitute honey for the sugar. Do *everything else* exactly the same way.

12. After you have recorded your last observation, draw your conclusions.

Rising Yeast

CONCLUSIONS

Explain what happened when you did not put yeast into the dough.

_____

_____

How did the amount of sugar affect how the dough rose?_____

_____

How did the amount of honey affect how the dough rose?_____

_____

Which had a greater effect on the yeast--sugar or honey? _____

_____

_____

Student Guide
Lesson 8: Kingdom Planta

Humans would not be able to survive without plants. We eat plants, such as lettuce, but so do the animals that may also become our food. Plants also supply us with the oxygen we breathe. Get ready for a journey through Kingdom Planta.

Lesson Objectives

- Identify characteristics common to organisms in Kingdom Planta (all except mosses are vascular, all use photosynthesis to get nutrients).
- Identify two plants in Kingdom Planta.
- Describe *vascular plants* as plants that have systems for transporting water, sugar, and minerals, whereas *nonvascular plants* lack these structures.
- Explain how sugar, water, and minerals are transported in vascular plants.
- Compare characteristics of gymnosperms and angiosperms.

PREPARE

Approximate lesson time is 60 minutes.

Advance Preparation

- You will need two fresh stalks of celery for the Up Goes the Water activity.

Materials

For the Student

Come Learn with Me: The Kingdoms of Life: Classification by Bridget Anderson

📖 Compare Angiosperms and Gymnosperms

📖 Up Goes the Water

celery - stalk (2)

Keywords and Pronunciation

angiosperm (AN-jee-uh-spuhrm)

gymnosperm (JIM-nuh-spuhrm)

Sequoia sempervirens (sih-KWOY-uh sem-puhr-VIY-ruhns)

LEARN
Activity 1: Let's Read *(Online)*

Plants come in all shapes and sizes. Some have leaves that change colors with the seasons. Some have bright flowers, and some have seeds. All belong to Kingdom Planta. Read pages 30 through 37 of *The Kingdoms of Life: Classification*.

Activity 2: Compare Angiosperms and Gymnosperms (Offline)

If you look carefully at the features of a tree, you can tell whether it is an angiosperm or a gymnosperm.

Activity 3: Up Goes the Water (Online)

Have you ever wondered exactly how--and how quickly--water can travel up the stem of a plant? A stalk of celery will give you the answer!

Safety

This activity involves working with food. Before letting your student handle the food, be certain he is not allergic to it.

ASSESS

Lesson Assessment: Kingdom Planta (Online)

You will complete an offline assessment covering the main objectives of this lesson. Your learning coach will score this assessment.

Name _____   Date _____

Compare Angiosperms and Gymnosperms

Do you remember the characteristics of angiosperms and gymno-sperms? Look at each characteristic listed in the table, then write YES if it applies and NO if it does not apply.

Characteristic	Angiosperms	Gymnosperms
Do they have seeds?		
Do they have flowers?		
Do most have needle or scale-like leaves?		
Do most have woody cones?		

Now that you have reviewed the characteristics, write a paragraph that compares angiosperms with gymnosperms. How are they alike? How are they different?

_____

_____

_____

_____

_____

_____

_____

_____

_____

_____

Name _____   Date _____

Up Goes the Water

Celery is a *vascular plant.* These types of plants have systems for transporting water, sugar, and minerals. In this experiment, you'll be able to watch the path the water takes.

Materials

2 fresh stalks of celery   knife
bowl   cooking syringe (baster)
2 drinking glasses   red food coloring
water   cutting board

Procedure

1. Place one stalk of celery into a bowl of water.

2 With adult help, carefully cut the lowermost part of the stalk while it is under water. This keeps air bubbles from entering the stem.

3. Put a drinking glass in the bowl of water and transfer the celery stalk under water into the glass.

4. Repeat the steps with the other stalk of celery.

5. Use a kitchen syringe (baster) to remove all but 4 cm of water from both glasses.

6. Add enough food coloring to one glass to make the water very dark.

7. Observe both stalks after three hours.

   What do you notice? _____

   _____

Up Goes the Water

8. Remove the stalk that has been exposed to the red food coloring and lay it on a cutting board.

9. Carefully cut the stalk 3 cm above the bottom. Can you see where the food coloring moved up the stem?

10. Continue to cut the stem every 3 cm and observe the stalk.

   What do you see? _____

   _____

   _____

Name: _____   Date: _____

Lesson Assessment

Kingdom Planta

1. Gymnosperms and angiosperms are both vascular plants within the Kingdom Planta. Which description is common to **both** gymnosperms and angiosperms?

   A. needle-like leaves

   B. seeds

   C. flowers

   D. woody Cones

2. Organisms from the Kingdom Planta are found throughout the environment around us. Mosses are members of this kingdom. Which organisms belong to the Kingdom Planta? Select the **two** correct answers.

   A. mushrooms

   B. redwood trees

   C. seaweed

   D. daisies

3. All of the organisms in the Kingdom Planta, except mosses, are vascular. Which description is common to all organisms in the Kingdom Planta?

   A. produce pollen

   B. have stamens and pistils

   C. produce cones

   D. use photosynthesis to get nutrients

4. What is the difference between vascular and nonvascular plants?

   A. presence of leaves

   B. need water in order to grow

   C. have systems for transporting water and minerals

5. How are water and minerals transported in vascular plants? Explain in a short paragraph that uses the terms *xylem*, *phloem*, and *shoots*.

_____

_____

_____

_____

_____

_____

Student Guide
Lesson 9: Kingdom Animalia

Worms, flamingoes, and bears, oh my! It's hard to imagine that all these organisms are part of Kingdom Animalia. I wonder what else you'll find in this diverse kingdom?

Lesson Objectives

- Identify characteristics common to organisms in Kingdom Animalia (multicellular, need to get food from an outside source).
- Identify two organisms in Kingdom Animalia that are vertebrates.
- Identify two organisms in Kingdom Animalia that are invertebrates.
- Recognize that Kingdom Animalia includes organisms that are vertebrates and invertebrates.

PREPARE

Approximate lesson time is 60 minutes.

Materials

> For the Student
>> Come Learn with Me: The Kingdoms of Life: Classification by Bridget Anderson

Keywords and Pronunciation
Animalia (A-nuh-MAY-lee-uh)

LEARN
Activity 1: Let's Read *(Online)*

Did you know that most animals do not have a backbone? Do you know how fish breathe? Discover the answers to these and many other questions. Read pages 38 through 45 of *The Kingdoms of Life: Classification*.

Activity 2: Learn More About Kingdom Animalia *(Online)*

ASSESS

Lesson Assessment: Kingdom Animalia (*Online*)

You will complete an online assessment covering the main goals of this lesson. Your assessment will be scored by the computer.

Student Guide
Lesson 10: Unit Review and Assessment

The seven levels of classification help us understand the many kinds of living things in the world. How can that knowledge be put to practical use? Find out!

Lesson Objectives
- Name the six kingdoms (Archaebacteria, Eubacteria, Protista, Fungi, Planta, and Animalia) and identify organisms from each.
- Demonstrate mastery of the skills taught in this unit.
- Explain how sugar, water, and minerals are transported in vascular plants.
- Recognize that living things are classified by shared characteristics, and that there are seven major levels of classification: kingdom, phylum, class, order, family, genus, and species.
- Compare the characteristics of the various groups of plants.

PREPARE

Approximate lesson time is 60 minutes.

Materials
For the Student
📖 Question Review Table

LEARN
Activity 1: The Carolus Linnaeus Zoological Garden (Online)
Most zoos concentrate on animals, but you've seen that there are five other kingdoms of living organisms. Help an architect plan a zoological garden that includes all the kingdoms.

ASSESS
Unit Assessment: Taxonomy of Plants and Animals (Online)
Complete an offline Unit Assessment. Your learning coach will score this part of the Assessment.

LEARN
Activity 2. Optional: Unit Assessment Review Table (Online)
If you earned a score of **less than 80%** on the Unit Assessment, complete the activity.
If you earned a score of **80% or greater**, you may skip this activity.

Let's prepare to retake the Unit Assessment:

- Print the Question Review Table.
- Identify the questions that you answered incorrectly.
- Complete the appropriate review activities listed in the table.

Note: This will guide you through the process of using the Unit Assessment Review Tables. You may skip this video if you've already viewed it in another unit or course. As always, check in with your student's teacher if you have any questions.

Activity 3. Optional: ZlugQuest Measurement *(Online)*

Name: _____   Date: _____

Unit Assessment

Taxonomy of Plants and Animals

Circle TRUE or FALSE.

1. TRUE or FALSE: Gymnosperms reproduce using seeds, but angiosperms do not.

2. TRUE or FALSE: Living things are classified by shared characteristics.

3. TRUE or FALSE: All gymnosperms lose their leaves in the winter.

4. Linnaeus created seven levels of classification. Circle the names of the seven levels.

Kingdom	Genus	Species	Class
Protista	Organism	Fungi	Family
Animalia	Order	Phylum	Line

5. The first two letters of each of the seven kingdoms have been provided. Complete the name of each kingdom, and then write the letter to match the kingdom with its description.

A. Pl_____

B. An_____

C. Eu_____

D. Ar_____

E. Pr_____

F. Fu_____

_____ Paramecium and algae

_____ Heterotroph

_____ Mushrooms and lichens

_____ Angiosperms and gymnosperms

_____ Fish, insects, and mammals

_____ Single-cell organisms such as halophiles

6. How do vascular plants get the water and minerals that they need to live and grow? Be sure to include the words *xylem*, *phloem*, and *roots* in your answer.

_____

_____

_____

_____

_____

_____

_____

_____

_____

_____

_____

Assessment Date

Unit 7: Taxonomy of Plants and Animals

Before you retake the Unit Assessment, use the table to figure out which activities you should review.

Question Review Table

Circle the numbers of the questions that you missed on the Unit Assessment. Review the activities that correspond with these questions.

Question	Lesson	Review Activity
1,3	8: Kingdom Planta	Let's Read Compare Gymnosperms and Angiosperms
2,4	2: The Tools of Taxonomy	Let's Read Identifying Trees Dichotomous Keys
5	3: Phylogenetic Trees and the Kingdoms of Life	Let's Read What Would Linnaeus Say?
6	8: Kingdom Planta	Let's Read Up Goes the Water

Student Guide
Lesson 1: The Miracle of Life

Do you ever wonder how the bodies of animals work? How are animals able to regulate their body temperatures? How do their coats change colors? These questions, and many more, are part of the area of study called *animal physiology*.

Lesson Objectives

- Recognize that all body systems play a role in maintaining a constant internal environment.
- Describe how bones and muscles interact to cause movement.

PREPARE

Approximate lesson time is 60 minutes.

Materials

> For the Student
>> Come Learn with Me: How Bodies Work: Animal Physiology by Bridget Anderson
>> 🖳 Cooling Effect

Keywords and Pronunciation

cell membrane : The fatty outer covering of a cell. The cell membrane allows certain substances to pass through it.

cytoplasm (SIY-tuh-pla-zuhm) : The jelly-like matter of a living cell that is outside the nucleus. Organelles are contained in cytoplasm.

homeostasis (HOH-mee-oh-STAY-suhs) : A state of balance reached through reactions within a cell or organism. Homeostatis is important for cells to function efficiently.

lysosomes (LIY-suh-sohm) : An organelle in animal cells that contains powerful enzymes. Lysosomes contain chemicals that process substances within the cell.

mitochondria (miy-tuh-KAHN-dree-uh) : The organelles that produce usable chemical energy. There can be many mitochondria in a single cell.

nutrient : Any substance that provides nourishment. Proteins are a type of nutrient for the body.

organelle (or-guh-NEL) : A tiny structure in the cytoplasm of the cell. Animal cells contain different types of organelles.

LEARN
Activity 1: Let's Read (Online)

How intelligent are animals? How do they respond to the world around them? Animal physiologists ask questions like these. Learn about the answers they find.

Activity 2: Cooling Effect (Offline)

How does your body cool itself when it is hot? This experiment will provide one answer.

ASSESS

Lesson Assessment: The Miracle of Life (Online)

You will complete an offline assessment covering the main objectives of this lesson. Your learning coach will score this assessment.

Name _____   Date _____

Cooling Effect

Do you know how your body cools down? This experiment will show you.

Materials

Thermometer   Clock
Cotton ball   Graduated cylinder
Rubbing alcohol 10mL

Procedure

1. Lay the thermometer on a table. Let it come to room temperature. Record the temperature on a piece of paper.
2. Moisten a cotton ball with rubbing alcohol.
3. Spread the cotton ball into thin strands. Spread a thin layer of the wet cotton across the bulb of the thermometer.
4. Blow across the wet cotton 15 times.
5. Record the temperature on the thermometer.

Conclusions

What happened to the temperature after adding the cotton ball with the rubbing alcohol?

_____

_____

How is this like the body's response when it gets too hot?

_____

_____

_____

_____

_____

_____

Name _____   Date _____

Miracle of Life Lesson Assessment

1. TRUE or FALSE: One body system maintains the constant internal environment of the whole body.   _____

2. Describe how muscles and bones work together to help the human body move. In your answer, be sure to include the words *muscles*, *bones*, *ligaments*, and *tendons*.

_____

_____

_____

_____

_____

_____

_____

_____

_____

Student Guide
Lesson 2: The Nervous and Endocrine Systems

The *nervous system* is the command center of an animal's body. This system helps maintain the homeostasis of the body. The hormones from the endocrine system also help to maintain a balance.

Lesson Objectives

- Identify the parts of the human nervous system and their function (brain, spinal chord, and nerves).
- Identify some parts of the human endocrine system and their function (pituitary gland, thyroid gland, adrenal gland, and pancreas).

PREPARE

Approximate lesson time is 60 minutes.

Materials

For the Student

Come Learn with Me: How Bodies Work: Animal Physiology by Bridget Anderson

💻 The Endocrine System

Keywords and Pronunciation

adrenal (uh-DREE-nl)

endocrine (EN-duh-kruhn)

gland : An organ that produces special chemicals called hormones. The adrenal glands produce adrenaline when the brain instructs them to do so.

motor neurons : Nerve cells that deliver orders from the brain and spinal chord telling the body what to do. Motor neurons tell the body when it needs to move.

nerve : A thin fiber that sends messages between the brain or spinal chord and other parts of the body. The optic nerve passes messages between the brain and the eye.

nerve cord : A strand of nerve tissue that runs the length of the body and forms the main part of an animal's nervous system. The spinal cord is an example of a nerve cord.

nerve net : A simple nervous system containing nerve cells but no brain. Some invertebrates, such as jellyfish, have a nerve net.

pancreas (PAN-kree-uhs)

pituitary (puh-TOO-uh-tair-ee)

sensory neurons : Nerve cells that gather information from the body and carry it to the brain and spinal chord. Sensory neurons alert the brain when the body is damaged in some way.

LEARN

Activity 1: Let's Read *(Online)*

The nervous system involves the brain and a huge network of nerves. It carries messages between the brain and the body. Did you know that the body also has chemical messengers? Hormones of the endocrine system are chemical messengers.

Activity 2: The Endocrine System *(Offline)*

What role does the endocrine system play in your body? Use *Come Learn With Me: How Bodies Work: Animal Physiology* and this article at Kid's Health: Your Endocrine SystemKid's Health: Your Endocrine System to learn about the glands and hormones that make up your endocrine system.

ASSESS

Lesson Assessment: The Nervous and Endocrine Systems (*Online*)

You will complete an online assessment covering the main objectives of this lesson. Your assessment will be scored by the computer.

Name _____   Date _____

The Endocrine System

Use the Word Bank to label the main structures of the endocrine system.

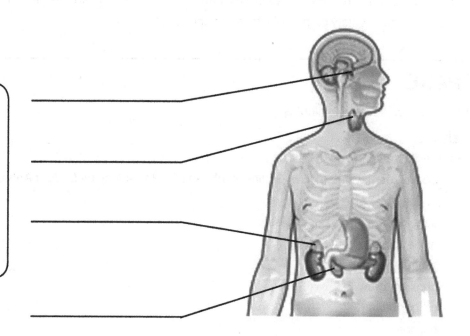

Word Bank

adrenal glands
thyroid
pituitary gland
pancreas

Describe the function of each gland here. Two have been completed for you.

1. Adrenal glands _____

_____

2. Thyroid gland **produces hormones that influence the growth and development of the body**_____

3. Pituitary gland **controls the growth of the human body, among other things**_____

4. Pancreas _____

_____

Student Guide
Lesson 3: The Respiratory System

Animals cannot survive without oxygen. But how does oxygen get into animal bodies? Learn more about the respiratory systems of animals and investigate for yourself!

Lesson Objectives

- Identify the parts of the human respiratory system (nose, mouth, trachea, lungs, diaphragm).
- Describe how the respiratory system exchanges carbon dioxide and oxygen in the lungs.
- Demonstrate mastery of the skills taught in this lesson.

PREPARE

Approximate lesson time is 60 minutes.

Materials

For the Student

Come Learn with Me: How Bodies Work: Animal Physiology by Bridget Anderson

📖 Lung Model

bag, clear plastic - zipper-closed

bottle, plastic - 2 Liter

clay - small ball

drinking straw

rubber band (3)

balloon

scissors, round-end safety

tape - masking

Keywords and Pronunciation

alveoli (al-VEE-uh-liy) : Tiny air sacs in each lung through which oxygen enters and carbon dioxide leaves the blood. Alveoli are shaped like bunches of grapes.

bronchi (BRONG-kiy) : The tubes in the lungs through which air passes. Human have two bronchi--one for each lung.

carbon dioxide : A gas with no color or smell that is a mixture of carbon and oxygen. Animals breathe out carbon dioxide.

diaphragm (DIY-uh-fram) : A dome-shaped muscle below the lungs that assists with breathing. When you breathe in, your diaphragm expands.

spiracle (SPIHR-uh-kuhl)

trachea (TRAY-kee-uh) : A tube in animals used for drawing air into the body. Air passes from the nose and mouth into the trachea.

LEARN

Activity 1: Let's Read *(Online)*

Your respiratory system is essential to every breath you take. It helps you speak, sing, and do many other things.

Activity 2: Lung Model *(Offline)*

What structures are part of the respiratory system? How does the respiratory system work? Build a model to test out your own hypothesis.

ASSESS

Lesson Assessment: The Respiratory System *(Offline)*

You will complete an offline assessment covering the main objectives of this lesson. Your learning coach will score this assessment.

Name   Date

The Lung Model

What structures are part of the respiratory system? Build a model
and test your own hypothesis.

Materials

2-liter plastic bottle   balloon
zipper-closed plastic bag   scissors
clay - 1 ball the size of a child's fist   1 drinking straw
3 rubber bands that can stretch across   masking tape
    the bottom of a 2-liter bottle

Procedure

To see how your lungs work, make a model lung.

1. Cut the bottom of a 2-liter plastic bottle at the point where the
   width is the same as its base. Keep the top part of the bottle for
   this model and discard the bottom part of the bottle.
2. Cut the zippered part off a sandwich bag. Using the top part of
   the bottle, place the bag around the bottom of the bottle. Hold the
   bag in place with a rubber band.
3. Place a straw into the neck of a balloon and use masking tape
   to seal it closed.
4. Remove the cap from the bottle. Hold the straw so that the
   balloon is inside the bottle.
5. Use clay to seal the opening of the bottle and hold the straw in
   place.
6. As you gently pull the plastic bag, the balloon "lung" will inflate
   by pulling air in through the straw (windpipe). When you gently
   push the bag back towards the bottle, the balloon will deflate.

The plastic bag acts like your *diaphragm*, a sheet-like muscle that
separates your chest area and abdomen. Your diaphragm moves
down when you inhale and back up when you exhale.

Conclusion

Use the back of this page to describe the exchange of oxygen and
carbon dioxide in the lungs.

Name: _____   Date: _____

Lesson Assessment

The Respiratory System

Circle the correct answer for each of the following.

1. What is the name of the large dome-shaped muscle under your lungs that helps you breathe?

    A. nose

    B. mouth

    C. trachea

    D. diaphragm

2. If your mouth is closed, which part of your respiratory system takes in air first as you breathe?

    A. nose

    B. mouth

    C. trachea

    D. diaphragm

3. What is the name of the long tube that runs from your mouth and connects to the lungs?

    A. nose

    B. mouth

    C. trachea

    D. diaphragm

4. Which part of the respiratory system, which also helps with food digestion, helps the body take in air?

    A. nose

    B. mouth

    C. trachea

    D. lungs

5. Which part of the respiratory system is the spongy organ that takes in air through the trachea?

   A. nose

   B. mouth

   C. trachea

   D. lungs

6. Describe how the respiratory system exchanges carbon dioxide and oxygen in the lungs. Use the words *carbon dioxide*, *lungs*, *trachea*, and *bronchi* in your answer.

   _____

   _____

   _____

   _____

   _____

   _____

   _____

   _____

Student Guide
Lesson 4: The Circulatory System

How do food and other materials move through the body? The transport system of the body, the *circulatory system,* is the key to it all! Hop on for a tour through the circulatory system.

Lesson Objectives

- Explain how blood flows through the human heart.
- Recognize that the circulatory system transports oxygen and nutrients to cells while carrying carbon dioxide and other wastes for removal.
- Recognize that some organisms have no circulatory system, some have an open circulatory system, and others have a closed circulatory system.
- Identify the structures of the heart (atria, ventricles, valves, major veins and arteries).
- Demonstrate mastery of the skills taught in this lesson.

PREPARE

Approximate lesson time is 60 minutes.

Materials

> For the Student
>
> > Come Learn with Me: How Bodies Work: Animal Physiology by Bridget Anderson
> >
> > 🖥 A Circulation Model

Keywords and Pronunciation

capillary : A small blood vessel that carries blood between the arteries and the veins. Capillaries are the smallest, thinnest blood vessels.

LEARN
Activity 1: Let's Read *(Online)*

A lot of movement goes on inside bodies. Blood, oxygen, nutrients, and certain wastes move from one part to another. The *circulatory system* is what makes that happen.

Activity 2: A Circulation Model *(Offline)*

Not all organisms have a closed circulatory system. Investigate another model of circulation-- the open circulatory system.

Activity 3: How Does Blood Flow Through a Human Heart? *(Online)*

The blood in the human heart follows a regular path. What changes happen to it as it follows the path of the many blood vessels and arteries? Explore a website to see a beating heart!

ASSESS

Lesson Assessment: The Circulatory System *(Online)*

You will complete an offline assessment covering the main objectives of this lesson. Your learning coach will score this assessment.

Name _____   Date _____

A Circulation Model

Not all organisms have a closed circulatory system. Investigate another model of circulation--the open circulatory system.

Materials
1 T. honey
1 drop of food coloring, any color
1 paper plate

Procedure
1 Place a spoonful of honey on a paper plate.
2. Add a drop of food coloring around one edge of the honey.
3. Gently tilt the paper plate to make the honey flow in different directions.

Conclusions
What happened to the food coloring? _____
_____

Compare this model to the open circulatory system. _____
_____
_____
_____
_____
_____

Would this circulatory system be efficient for a human? Why or why not? _____
_____
_____
_____
_____

Name: _____   Date: _____

Lesson Assessment

The Circulatory System

Circle the correct answer for each.

1. TRUE or FALSE: All organisms have a closed circulatory system.

    A. True

    B. False

2. Which structure of the heart acts like an automatic door that closes once blood enters a chamber and forces it to exit in the proper direction.

    A. atria

    B. calves

    C. arteries

    D. ventricles

3. Which part of the heart takes blood from the veins and pumps it into a ventricle?

    A. atria

    B. valves

    C. arteries

    D. ventricles

4. What is the name of one of the lower chambers of the heart that receives blood from the upper chambers and pumps it into the arteries?

    A. atria

    B. valves

    C. arteries

    D. ventricles

5. What is the name of the blood vessels that carry blood from the heart to all the other parts of the body?

   A. atria

   B. valves

   C. arteries

   D. ventricles

6. The circulatory system transports oxygen and nutrients to cells of the body. What does it remove from the body?

   A. oxygen

   B. carbon dioxide and other wastes

   C. blood

   D. capillaries

7. Explain how blood flows through the human heart. Be sure to include the words *lung, valve, atrium*, and *blood* in your answer.

   _____

   _____

   _____

   _____

   _____

   _____

   _____

   _____

   _____

Student Guide
Lesson 5: The Digestive System

How does food you eat get to all parts of your body? Your digestive system plays a key role in getting nutrients into your blood and wastes out of your body.

Lesson Objectives

- Sequence the digestion process.
- Identify the structures involved in the digestive process and describe their function (mouth, esophagus, stomach, small intestine, large intestine, and liver).
- Demonstrate mastery of the skills taught in this lesson.

PREPARE

Approximate lesson time is 60 minutes.

Materials

For the Student

Come Learn with Me: How Bodies Work: Animal Physiology by Bridget Anderson

Optional

📠 Folds

glass container, large - slender

paper towels (5)

tape - masking

Keywords and Pronunciation

enzymes (EN-ziym) : A protein in the body. Some enzymes help break food down into usable nutrients during digestion. Enzymes in your saliva break down starch, starting the process of digestion.

esophagus (ih-SAH-fuh-guhs)

peristalsis (pair-uh-STAWL-suhs) : Muscle contractions that move food, waste, and other contents through some digestive organs in the body. Peristalsis of the esophagus helps you swallow food.

vacuole (VA-kyuh-wohl) : A storage organelle of the cell. Some vacuoles help transport food molecules across a cell membrane.

LEARN
Activity 1: Let's Read *(Online)*

All animals need to take in food. The digestive system breaks down food and gets it into the blood for distribution to the body's cells. The same system helps the body get rid of what it doesn't need.

Activity 2: The Parts of the Digestive System *(Online)*

What structures are part of your digestive system? Some of them might surprise you!

ASSESS

Lesson Assessment: The Digestive System (*Online*)

You will complete an offline assessment covering the main objectives of this lesson. Your learning coach will score this assessment.

LEARN

Activity 3. Optional: Folds *(Offline)*

This activity is OPTIONAL. It's provided for enrichment or extra practice, but not required for completion of this lesson. You may skip this activity.

The intestines have to absorb a lot of nutrients. How do they do this efficiently? You may find the answer in some paper towels.

Name _____   Date _____

Lesson Assessment

Circle the correct answer for each.

1. Which part of the human body begins to break down food first?
   A. small intestine
   B. liver
   C. mouth
   D. esophagus

2. Which long tube carries food from the mouth to the stomach?
   A. small intestine
   B. liver
   C. mouth
   D. esophagus

3. What is the name of the muscular, sac-shaped organ located below the liver where food is digested?
   A. small intestine
   B. stomach
   C. mouth
   D. esophagus

4. What is the name of the long, coiled part of the digestive system connected to the stomach that finishes digesting the last bits of food?
   A. small intestine
   B. liver
   C. mouth
   D. esophagus

5. Which large organ in the human body located above the stomach helps digest food and clean the blood?
   A. trachea
   B. liver
   C. mouth
   D. large intestine

Name _____   Date _____

Lesson Assessment

6. What is the name of the thick, lower end of the digestive tract where solid waste is gathered and leaves the body?
   A. trachea
   B. liver
   C. mouth
   D. large intestine

7. Place the following steps of digestion in the correct order. Label the first step of digestion A, the second step B, and so forth. (1 point each)

   _____ The remaining food passes into the large intestine. Water is absorbed from the large intestine and the rest of the material is stored as solid waste.

   _____ Saliva rushes into the mouth and mixes with the broken-down food.

   _____ The food travels down the esophagus.

   _____ The teeth in the mouth bite off a piece of food. The teeth continue to break the food into smaller pieces.

   _____ The muscles of the stomach churn the food and continue to break it down.

   _____ The broken down food, called *chyme*, enters the small intestine.

Name _____   Date _____

Folds

In some ways, folded sheets of paper towels act just like the tissues inside the human intestines. How do you think they're similar? State your hypothesis, then test it.

Materials
5 paper towels
Slender glass jar
Masking tape

Procedure
1. Tape one piece of masking tape down the full length of the jar.
2. Fill the jar three-quarters of the way full with water.
3. With a pen, mark the level of the water on the tape.
4. Fold one sheet of paper towels in half four times.
5. Place the paper towel into the jar, making sure it is under water.
6. Remove the wet paper towel from the jar.
7. Mark the new water level on the tape.
8. Lay four sheets of paper towels on top of each other and fold them in half four times.
9. Dip the paper into the water, making sure it is under water.
10. Remove the paper towel and mark the water level.

Observations
What did you notice? _____

_____

_____

In which ways did the folded paper towels act like human intestines?

_____

_____

_____

_____

_____

Student Guide
Lesson 6: The Excretory System

Your body produces wastes that are not useful and need to be removed. Your lungs get rid of the carbon dioxide that was created in your body through cellular respiration. What other wastes are in your body, and what systems remove them? Learn about the special filters and transport systems as you investigate the excretory system of the body.

Lesson Objectives

- Identify the organs of the excretory system and describe their function (lungs, liver, kidneys, and skin).
- Explain how the excretory system removes cellular waste from the blood, converts it to urine, and stores it in the bladder before it leaves the body.
- Demonstrate mastery of the skills taught in this lesson.

PREPARE

Approximate lesson time is 60 minutes.

Materials

For the Student

    Come Learn with Me: How Bodies Work: Animal Physiology by Bridget Anderson

    🖳 Excretory System Crossword Puzzle

Keywords and Pronunciation

bladder : The organ that stores liquid waste before it leaves the body. The bladder can stretch to hold about a pint of urine.

nephron (NEH-frahn) : A tiny fiber in the kidney in which the filtering of water and waste from the blood takes place. There are approximately one million nephrons in one of your kidneys.

ureter (YUHR-uh-tuhr)

ureter tube (YUHR-uh-tuhr) : A tube through which urea is transported from the kidneys to the bladder. A valve at the base of the ureter tube prevents urine from flowing back into the kidney.

LEARN

Activity 1: Let's Read (Online)

Everyone's body produces wastes--and everyone needs a way to get rid of those wastes. The excretory system is designed to handle some of the waste-removal problems.

Activity 2: The Excretory System Crossword Puzzle (Offline)

Solve a crossword puzzle based on the excretory system.

ASSESS

Lesson Assessment: The Excretory System (Online)

You will complete an offline assessment covering the main objectives of this lesson. Your learning coach will score this assessment.

Name _____   Date _____

Excretory System Crossword Puzzle

Use the clues on the next page to complete the puzzle.

Excretory System Crossword Puzzle

ACROSS

1. This expandable, sac-like organ holds urine in the body.
2. Animals with one-way digestive systems get rid of wastes through this opening.
6. This gas waste is produced by cells. It leaves the body through breathing organs and structures.
8. This liquid waste is passed through the pores of the skin. It is a part of sweat.
9 This general name is given to material that is not useful to the body and must be removed.
13. This is the tube through which urine leaves the body.
15. Cow feces, which many farmers use to fertilize fields, are given this term.
16. This is a combination of urea, water, and salt.
17. The bladder sits between these bones.

DOWN

1. Feces are usually a combination of old cells, ___, water, and leftover chemicals.
3. This system filters waste from the blood, stores it, and gets rid of it.
4. This organ filters blood.
5. This is the scientific name for solid waste.
7. These surround the bladder. They expand when the bladder is full, then contract to release urine down the urethra.
10. This is the number of kidneys in the human body.
11. This is the name for the tiny filter in the kidneys.
12. Animals with ___-way digestive systems get rid of their wastes through the same opening in which they eat food.
13. Urine flows through _____ tubes to the bladder.
14. This is the name for liquid waste that passes through the kidneys.

Name _____   Date _____

The Excretory System Lesson Assessment

Circle the correct answer for each question.

1. Carbon dioxide is a waste product from breathing. Which organ of the body, which is attached to the trachea, pushes carbon dioxide out of the body?
   - A. liver
   - B. lungs
   - C. kidney
   - D. skin

2. Which organ, located just below the diaphragm, turns waste materials from the blood into urea?
   - A. liver
   - B. lungs
   - C. kidney
   - D. skin

3. Which organ releases salt and liquid waste from the body through its pores and glands?
   - A. liver
   - B. lungs
   - C. kidney
   - D. skin

4. Which pair of organs, located in the lower back, collects liquid and waste from the blood?
   - A. liver
   - B. lungs
   - C. kidneys
   - D. skin

Name   Date

The Excretory System Lesson Assessment

5. How does the human urinary system filter waste from the blood,
    store it and then get rid of it? Please include the word *kidneys*,
    urine, and *bladder* in your answer.

_____

_____

_____

_____

_____

_____

_____

Student Guide
Lesson 7: The Immune System and the Reproductive System

How does the human body protect itself from disease? Learn about the immune system as it "fights" to protect your body from disease and illness.

Lesson Objectives

- Describe some reproduction differences between animals.
- Identify the structures involved with the immune system and describe their function (bone marrow, white blood cells, and lymphocytes).
- Identify two ways we can work to keep our immune system healthy (get vaccines, eat healthful foods).
- Recognize that different organisms reproduce through division or fusion.

PREPARE

Approximate lesson time is 60 minutes.

Materials

> For the Student
>
> > Come Learn with Me: How Bodies Work: Animal Physiology by Bridget Anderson
>
> 🖳 Immune and Reproductive System Riddles

Keywords and Pronunciation

antibody : A protein that fights infection. Lymphocytes manufacture antibodies to protect the body against disease.

blood marrow : A soft, reddish substance that is inside bones and produces blood cells. Doctors sometimes examine blood marrow to check on the immune system's health.

lymphocyte (LIMP-fuh-siyt) : A kind of white blood cell that produces antibodies to fight infection. Lymphocytes recognize different types of infection, and then send the correct antibodies to fight the infection.

pathogen (PA-thuh-jen) : Something that can cause a disease. Bacteria is a pathogen.

vaccine (vak-SEEN) : A substance containing weakened, dead, or living organisms that causes a body's immune system to fight against disease. The vaccine against polio is so effective that disease has been eliminated in many countries.

white blood cell : A colorless blood cell that is part of the body's immune system. A white blood cell protects the body against infection.

LEARN
Activity 1: Let's Read (Online)

The immune system is like an army. It is designed to fight anything that tries to attack the body. Learn how this army works.

Activity 2: Immune and Reproductive System Riddles (Online)

It's riddle time! Solve this collection of immune and reproductive system riddles.

ASSESS

Lesson Assessment: The Immune System and the Reproductive System

(Online)

You will complete an online assessment covering the main objectives of this lesson. Your assessment will be scored by the computer.

Name _____   Date _____

Immune and Reproductive System Riddles

Read each riddle, then solve it. (Hint: You'll find help in your text.)

1. Animal life continues because of me. I am the system by which animals create new life. What am I? _____

2. I am an animal that splits up into pieces, making copies of myself in order to reproduce. What am I? _____

3. Some animals, such as a sea anemone, reproduce by division. But I am a different form of reproduction in which two cells from two animals of the same species join together to form a new animal. What form of reproduction am I? _____

4. Animals' bodies are designed to protect against things like me. I also called a "germ." What am I? _____

5. When an animal gets sick, I start producing lots of white blood cells. What am I? _____

6. I am made of many layers and am the first line of an animal's defense against germs. What am I? _____

7. I am a type of medicine that teaches an animal's body to produce antibodies ahead of time. What am I? _____

8. I am made in an animal's bone marrow. I move around an animal's body through the bloodstream, and I am also the second line of defense against germs. What am I? _____

9. I am one type of white blood cell that can remember the pathogens I come in contact with. I help other white blood cells find germs by creating antibodies that attach to the germs. What am I? _____

10. I am made of many tissues, organs, and systems including the reproductive and immune systems. These parts and systems work together to help me function. What am I? _____

Student Guide
Lesson 8: Unit Review and Assessment

A good knowledge of animal physiology is important even if you don't plan a career in medicine. Do you have a good understanding of how animals work? Here's your chance to find out!

Lesson Objectives

- Recognize that all body systems play a role in maintaining a constant internal environment.
- Explain how blood flows through the human heart.
- Describe how the respiratory system exchanges carbon dioxide and oxygen in the lungs.
- Explain how the excretory system removes cellular waste from the blood, converts it to urine, and stores it in the bladder before it leaves the body.
- Recognize that the circulatory system transports oxygen and nutrients to cells while removing carbon dioxide and other wastes.
- Put the steps of digestion in the correct order and describe the function of the structures that are part of the digestive process.
- Describe the functions of the immune system.
- Describe the reproductive system of some animals.

PREPARE

Approximate lesson time is 60 minutes.

Materials

For the Student

Come Learn with Me: How Bodies Work: Animal Physiology by Bridget Anderson

📖 Question Review Table

LEARN
Activity 1: Animal Physiology Unit Review (Online)

Have you ever considered being a doctor or a veterinarian? To do either, you need a good understanding of physiology. You already know the basics.

Imagine that you're applying for a part-time job in a veterinarian's office. Do you think you could qualify? Find out!

ASSESS
Unit Assessment: Animal Physiology (*Online*)
Complete an offline Unit Assessment. Your learning coach will score this part of the Assessment.

LEARN
Activity 2. Optional: Unit Assessment Review Table (*Online*)
If you earned a score of **less than 80%** on the Unit Assessment, complete the activity.

If you earned a score of **80% or greater**, you may skip this activity.

Let's prepare to retake the Unit Assessment:

- Print the Question Review Table.
- Identify the questions that you answered incorrectly.
- Complete the appropriate review activities listed in the table.

Note: This will guide you through the process of using the Unit Assessment Review Tables. You may skip this video if you've already viewed it in another unit or course. As always, check in with your student's teacher if you have any questions.

Name: _____ Date: _____

Unit Assessment

Animal Physiology

Circle the correct answer for questions 1 to 3.

1. TRUE or FALSE: All body systems help maintain the constant internal environment of the body.

2. Organisms reproduce by two main methods. One is division, where the animal divides and creates an exact copy of itself. What is the other main method of reproduction?

   A. combination

   B. fusion

   C. division

   D. fission

3. Which of the following are functions of the immune system? Select the **three** correct answers.

   A. Bones produce extra white blood cells to increase its defense against germs.

   B. The body filters the blood for waste materials.

   C. Cell membrane keeps germs from entering the cell.

   D. Lymphocytes create antibodies that attach to the germ.

Read each question and write your answer below.

4. Describe how the respiratory system exchanges carbon dioxide and oxygen in the lungs. Include the words *carbon dioxide*, *lungs*, *trachea* and *bronchi* in your answer.

   _____

   _____

   _____

   _____

   _____

   _____

5. Explain how blood flows through the human heart. Be sure to include the words *lung*, *valve*, *atrium* and *blood* in your answer.

_____

_____

_____

_____

_____

6. How does the human excretory system filter waste from the blood, store it and then get rid of it? Include the words *kidneys*, *urine* and *bladder* in your answer.

_____

_____

_____

_____

_____

7. Sequence the following steps of digestion. Label the first step of digestion 1.

_____ The remaining food passes into the large intestine. Water is absorbed from the large intestine and the rest of the material is stored as solid waste.

_____ Saliva rushes into the mouth and mixes with the broken down food.

_____ The broken down food, called chyme, enters the small intestine.

_____ The food travels down the esophagus.

_____ The muscles of the stomach churn the food and continue to break it down.

_____ The teeth in the mouth bite off a piece of food. The teeth continue to break the food into smaller pieces.

Assessment Date _____

Unit 8: Animal Physiology

Before you retake the Unit Assessment, use the table to figure out which activities you should review.

Question Review Table

Circle the numbers of the questions that you missed on the Unit Assessment. Review the activities that correspond with these questions.

Question	Lesson	Review Activity
1	1: The Miracle of Life	Let's Read Cooling Effect
2,3	7: The Immune System and the Reproductive System	Let's Read Immune and Reproductive System Riddles
4	3: The Respiratory System	Let's Read Lung Model
5	4: The Circulatory System	Let's Read A Circulation Model
6	6: The Excretory System	Let's Read The Excretory System Crossword Puzzle
7	5: The Digestive System	Let's Read The Parts of the Digestive System Folds

Student Guide
Lesson 9: Semester Review and Assessment

Do you know the difference between the chemical symbol Co and the compound CO_2? Do you understand how plants make their own food or how cells function? Take the semester assessment to show what you know. Get in touch with your respiratory and circulatory systems by taking deep breaths to calm your beating heart. You've worked hard this semester and are now ready to show you are the smartest member of Kingdom Anamalia!

Lesson Objectives

- Demonstrate mastery of the semester's content.
- Identify the three main parts of atoms as protons, electrons, and neutrons, and that protons have a positive charge, electrons a negative charge, and neutrons have no charge at all.
- Find the number of protons, electrons, and neutrons in an atom using its atomic number (the number of protons) and mass number (the number of protons and neutrons).
- Use the chemical formula of a compound to identify the elements from which it is composed, and determine the number of each type of atom in the compound.
- Identify the major structures of the cell (such as cell membrane, cytoplasm, and nucleus) and describe their functions.
- Describe the process of *photosynthesis* in plants.
- Explain that traits are passed from parents to offspring and are determined by genes, with an individual having two copies of each gene, one from each parent.
- Name the six kingdoms (Archaebacteria, Eubacteria, Protista, Fungi, Planta, and Animalia) and identify organisms from each.
- Explain how blood flows through the human heart.
- Describe the current model of the atom as a positively charged nucleus containing the protons and neutrons surrounded by electrons moving in certain regions within an "electron cloud".
- Identify four ways to increase the rate of some kinds of chemical reactions (increase the temperature, surface area, concentration, and add a catalyst).
- Use the pH scale to determine whether a solution is acidic or basic.
- Describe how reaction rates increase with temperature, surface area, concentration, and in the presence of a catalyst.
- Recognize the major cell organelles (for example, endoplasmic reticulum, ribosomes, Golgi bodies, chloroplasts, chromosomes, mitochondria, and vacuoles) and describe their functions.
- Define *diffusion* as the process by which molecules move from areas of higher concentration to areas of lower concentration.
- Recognize that water moves through membranes by *osmosis*--diffusion of water through a semipermeable membrane.
- Explain that different types of substances move across the cell membrane by means of diffusion, osmosis, and active transport.
- Identify the seven major levels of classification: Kingdom, Phylum, Class, Order, Family, Genus, and Species.
- Identify one organism in Kingdom Archaebacteria.
- Identify one organism in Kingdom Eubacteria.

- Identify two characteristics common to organisms in Kingdom Protista (thrive in wet environments, most are single celled).
- Identify two organisms in Kingdom Fungi (mushroom, lichens, some molds, yeast).
- Identify two plants in Kingdom Planta.
- Identify two organisms in Kingdom Animalia that are vertebrates.
- Identify the parts of the human respiratory system (nose, mouth, trachea, lungs, diaphragm).
- Describe how the respiratory system exchanges carbon dioxide and oxygen in the lungs.
- Recognize that the circulatory system transports oxygen and nutrients to cells while carrying carbon dioxide and other wastes for removal.
- Identify the structures of the heart (atria, ventricles, valves, major veins and arteries).
- Identify the organs of the excretory system and describe their function (lungs, liver, kidneys, and skin).
- Explain how the excretory system removes cellular waste from the blood, converts it to urine, and stores it in the bladder before it leaves the body.

PREPARE

Approximate lesson time is 60 minutes.

Materials

For the Student

📖 Periodic Table

Come Learn with Me: How Bodies Work: Animal Physiology by Bridget Anderson

Come Learn with Me: The Kingdoms of Life: Classification by Bridget Anderson

pencil (2)

LEARN
Activity 1: Semester Review (Online)

Review concepts and skills you have learned this semester. Click the arrow to continue.

ASSESS

Semester Assessment: Science 5, Semester 2 (Online)

Complete an offline Semester Assessment. Your learning coach will score this part of the assessment.

LEARN
Activity 2. Optional: ZlugQuest Measurement (Online)

Periodic Table of the Elements

1	2	3	4	5	6	7	8	9	10	11	12	13	14	15	16	17	18
hydrogen 1 **H** 1.00																	helium 2 **He** 4.00
lithium 3 **Li** 6.94	beryllium 4 **Be** 9.01											boron 5 **B** 10.81	carbon 6 **C** 10.01	nitrogen 7 **N** 14.01	oxygen 8 **O** 15.00	fluorine 9 **F** 18.00	neon 10 **Ne** 20.18
sodium 11 **Na** 22.99	magnesium 12 **Mg** 24.31											aluminum 13 **Al** 26.98	silicon 14 **Si** 28.09	phosphorus 15 **P** 30.97	sulfur 16 **S** 32.07	chlorine 17 **Cl** 35.45	argon 18 **Ar** 39.95
potassium 19 **K** 39.10	calcium 20 **Ca** 40.08	scandium 21 **Sc** 44.96	titanium 22 **Ti** 47.87	vanadium 23 **V** 50.94	chromium 24 **Cr** 51.97	manganese 25 **Mn** 54.94	iron 26 **Fe** 55.85	cobalt 27 **Co** 58.93	nickel 28 **Ni** 58.69	copper 29 **Cu** 63.55	zinc 30 **Zn** 65.41	gallium 31 **Ga** 69.72	germanium 32 **Ge** 72.64	arsenic 33 **As** 74.92	selenium 34 **Se** 78.96	bromine 35 **Br** 79.90	krypton 36 **Kr** 83.80
rubidium 37 **Rb** 85.47	strontium 38 **Sr** 87.62	yttrium 39 **Y** 88.91	zirconium 40 **Zr** 91.22	niobium 41 **Nb** 92.91	molybdenum 42 **Mo** 95.94	technetium 43 **Tc** 98	ruthenium 44 **Ru** 101.07	rhodium 45 **Rh** 102.91	palladium 46 **Pd** 106.42	silver 47 **Ag** 107.87	cadmium 48 **Cd** 112.41	indium 49 **In** 114.82	tin 50 **Sn** 118.71	antimony 51 **Sb** 121.76	tellurium 52 **Te** 127.60	iodine 53 **I** 126.90	xenon 54 **Xe** 131.29
cesium 55 **Cs** 132.91	barium 56 **Ba** 137.33	lanthanum 57 **La** 138.91	hafnium 72 **Hf** 178.49	tantalum 73 **Ta** 180.95	tungsten 74 **W** 183.84	rhenium 75 **Re** 186.21	osmium 76 **Os** 190.23	iridium 77 **Ir** 192.22	platinum 78 **Pt** 195.08	gold 79 **Au** 196.97	mercury 80 **Hg** 200.59	thallium 81 **Tl** 204.38	lead 82 **Pb** 207.2	bismuth 83 **Bi** 208.98	polonium 84 **Po** 209	astatine 85 **At** 210	radon 86 **Rn** 222
francium 87 **Fr** 223.00	radium 88 **Ra** 226.00	actinium 89 **Ac** 227.00	rutherfordium 104 **Rf** 261.00	dubnium 105 **Db** 262.00	seaborgium 106 **Sg** 266.00	bohrium 107 **Bh** 264.00	hassium 108 **Hs** 269.00	meitnerium 109 **Mt** 268.00	ununnilium 110 **Uun** 271.00	unununium 111 **Uuu** 272.00	ununbium 112 **Uub** 285.00		ununquadium 114 **Uuq** 289.00		ununhexium 116 **Uuh** ??????		ununoctium 118 **Uuo** ??????

cerium 58 **Ce** 140.12	praseodymium 59 **Pr** 140.91	neodymium 60 **Nd** 144.24	promethium 61 **Pm** 145	samarium 62 **Sm** 150.36	europium 63 **Eu** 151.96	gadolinium 64 **Gd** 157.25	terbium 65 **Tb** 158.93	dysprosium 66 **Dy** 162.50	holmium 67 **Ho** 164.93	erbium 68 **Er** 167.26	thulium 69 **Tm** 168.93	ytterbium 70 **Yb** 173.04	lutetium 71 **Lu** 174.97
thorium 90 **Th** 232.04	protactinium 91 **Pa** 231.04	uranium 92 **U** 238.03	neptunium 93 **Np** 237	plutonium 94 **Pu** 244	americium 95 **Am** 243	curium 96 **Cm** 247	berkelium 97 **Bk** 247.00	californium 98 **Cf** 251.00	einsteinium 99 **Es** 252.00	fermium 100 **Fm** 257.00	mendelevium 101 **Md** 258.00	nobelium 102 **No** 259.00	lawrencium 103 **Lr** 262.00

Name: _____   Date: _____

Semester Assessment

Select the answer that best completes the sentence.

1. Movement of molecules from an area of higher concentration to one of lower concentration is called _____.

    A. osmosis

    B. mitosis

    C. diffusion

    D. active transport

2. Movement of molecules from an area of lower concentration to one of higher concentration with energy is called _____.

    A. osmosis

    B. mitosis

    C. diffusion

    D. active transport

3. Movement of water across a membrane is called _____.

    A. osmosis

    B. mitosis

    C. diffusion

    D. active transport

4. Plant cells change the sun's energy to chemical energy during _____.

    A. meiosis

    B. mitosis

    C. photosynthesis

    D. active transport

5. One way to speed up a chemical reaction is to add a _____, which is unaffected by the reaction.

    A. catalyst

    B. surface area

    C. concentration

    D. heat

6. Increasing the _____ of a reactant exposes more of it to the reaction taking place.

    A. catalyst

    B. surface area

    C. concentration

    D. heat

7. What is the circulatory system's function?

    A. It removes cellular waste from the blood and converts it to urine.

    B. It exchanges carbon dioxide and oxygen in the lungs.

    C. It transports oxygen and nutrients to cells while removing carbon dioxide and other wastes.

    D. It breaks down food into usable nutrients.

8. Which organism belongs to the Kingdom Archaebacteria?

    A. halophile bacteria

    B. virus

    C. sea star

    D. worm

9. Which organism belongs to the Kingdom Eubacteria?

    A. thermophile bacteria

    B. paramecium

    C. cyanobacteria

    D. algae

10. Which organisms belong to the Kingdom Protista? Select the **two** correct answers.

   A. amoeba

   B. sea anemone

   C. beetle

   D. seaweed

11. Which organisms belong to the Kingdom Fungi? Select the **two** correct answers.

   A. pine tree

   B. mushroom

   C. moss

   D. mold

12. Which organisms belong to the Kingdom Planta? Select the **two** correct answers.

   A. moss

   B. lichens

   C. fern

   D. virus

13. Which organisms belong to the Kingdom Animalia? Select the **two** correct answers.

   A. frog

   B. mushroom

   C. worm

   D. thermophile bacteria

True or False. Write True or False on the line next to the statement.

14. _____ Chemicals packed together tightly react more slowly.

15. _____ Chemical reactions usually take place more quickly at high temperatures.

16. Match each cell part to its function.

cytoplasm

nucleus

cell membrane

chloroplasts

chromosome

A. in plant cells, converts energy from the sun into glucose.

B. contains all of the genetic information in a cell

C. directs all of the cell activities

D. holds all of the cells organelles

E. fluid-filled bubble responsible for getting rid of waste

F. controls what goes in and out of the cell

Fill in the blank with the word or words that best completes the sentence.

Word Bank

protons	genes	pH scale	siblings
electrons	neutrons	periodic table	interphase

17. The nucleus of an atom is made of _____ and
_____.

18. The _____ is used to indicate whether a solution is acidic or basic.

19. Traits passed down from parent to offspring are determined by
_____.

20. The nucleus of an atom is surrounded by _____.

21. Label the three main parts of an atom. Then describe their charges.

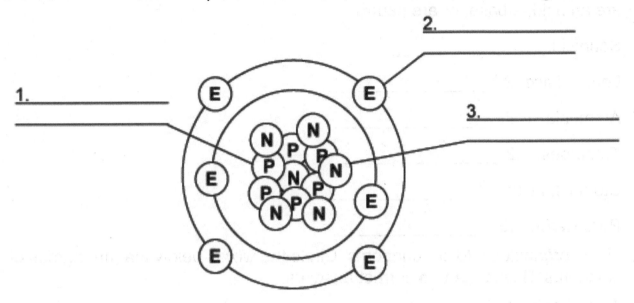

2. _____

_____

1. _____

3. _____

Identify the elements and the number of atoms of each in the chemical formulas.

22. $C_{12}H_{22}O_{11}$ _____

23. $PbSO_4$ _____

Write the compound for the formula described.

24. 1 atom of cobalt   _____
2 atoms of chlorine

25. 2 atoms of aluminum   _____
3 atoms of sulfur

26. Name two ways the properties of iron and oxygen are different from the compound iron oxide (rust).

_____

_____

27. An atom of platinum, Pt, has 78 protons. How many electrons does it contain? _____

28. Read the list of items and their pH. Classify them according to whether they are an acid, a base, or are neutral.

Soap: 11 _____

Lemon juice: 2.3 _____

Ammonia: 11.5 _____

Tomatoes: 4.2 _____

Stomach acid: 1.4 _____

Pure water: 7.0 _____

29. Life is organized into six kingdoms. Circle the words below that are names of kingdoms. Select the **two** correct answers.

A. Archaebacteria

B. Species

C. Vertebrate

D. Vascular Plants

E. Fungi

30. Life is organized into six kingdoms. Circle the words below that are names of kingdoms. Select the **two** correct answers.

A. Eubacteria

B. Planta

C. Protista

D. Animalia

E. Invertebrate

F. Non-vascular plants

31. Circle the words below that name major levels of classification. Select the **three** correct answers.

    A. family

    B. kingdom

    C. gender

    D. class

    E. phenotype

32. Circle the words below that name major levels of classification. Select the **four** correct answers.

    A. phylum

    B. species

    C. order

    D. genus

    E. group

33. Explain how blood flows through the human heart. Be sure to include the words lungs, atrium, and blood in your answer.

    _____

    _____

    _____

    _____

    _____